I'M NOT PERFECT. CAN I STILL GO TO HEAVEN?

I'M NOT PERFECT. CAN I STILL GO TO HEAVEN?

FINDING HOPE FOR THE CELESTIAL KINGDOM THROUGH THE ATONEMENT OF CHRIST

ANTHONY SWEAT

DESERET
BOOK

Salt Lake City, Utah

To the imperfect yet faithful: there is hope

Interior icons by Kayla Hackett and iStock Images.

Visit us at DeseretBook.com

Library of Congress Cataloging-in-Publication Data
Sweat, Anthony.
   I'm not perfect. Can I still go to heaven? : finding hope for the
Celestial Kingdom through the atonement of Christ / Anthony Sweat.
      p.   cm.
   Includes bibliographical references and index.
   ISBN 978-1-60641-231-2 (paperbound)
   1. Future life—The Church of Jesus Christ of Latter-day Saints.   2. Atonement—The Church of Jesus Christ of Latter-day Saints.   3. The Church of Jesus Christ of Latter-day Saints—Doctrines.   I. Title.
   BX8643.F87S94 2010
   234'.5—dc22   2009042226

Printed in the United States of America
Malloy Lithographing Incorporated, Ann Arbor, MI

10 9 8 7 6 5 4 3 2 1

CONTENTS

PREFACE

When I was a teenager, I was afraid to die. Not necessarily because my life would be cut short, nor because of the unknown of the next life. No, the problem wasn't the unknown of the next life; it was what I knew about the next life—or at least what I thought I knew. I was a teenaged boy who had made some mistakes—a young man who was still trying to figure things out. I was fearful that if I were suddenly called to stand before God to be judged, my sins would condemn me to a lesser kingdom, forever separating me from my earthly family and God's heavenly home. For this same reason, I was afraid of the Second Coming of Jesus Christ as well. I just knew I would be burned to stubble if He appeared suddenly as I walked between classes at school. Nor did I like it much in Sunday School or seminary when we had lessons on who qualifies for the celestial kingdom because, surely, I knew it wouldn't be me. Just as the teenaged Joseph Smith, "I often felt condemned for my weakness and imperfections" (Joseph Smith–History 1:29). I simply felt that I had made too many mistakes to ever think of making it to the celestial kingdom. I wasn't perfect, so I just knew I wasn't going to heaven. And I wasn't alone in my thinking.

As a religious educator, I interact with LDS youth almost every day. I've been fortunate to teach teenagers in gospel classes in a wide variety of places and circumstances. As I've taught these faithful youth, I've asked many of them to answer this simple question: If you died and were judged today, which kingdom do you feel you would go to? Their anonymous answers are generally the same: about half of them think they'll go to the celestial kingdom, and half of them don't. Here is the breakdown from a 2009 study involving 701 teenagers*:

52.8%=celestial kingdom

40.1%=terrestrial kingdom

5.1%=telestial kingdom

2.0%=outer darkness

These numbers are disheartening to me because the youth who took these surveys appear to be actively engaged in the gospel: regularly attending church and Mutual, serving in Church callings, and enrolling in programs such as seminary and Especially for Youth. These teenagers are the kind of kids who consistently read their scriptures, pray, and try their best to keep the commandments and do what is right. Yet half don't think they are celestial material. Why is this so?

The most common answer I hear from these youth goes something like this: "Well, I have sins and I'm not perfect, so I don't think I am good enough to go to the celestial kingdom. But I don't think I'm so terrible that I will go the telestial kingdom either. So I think I will end up somewhere in the middle, in the terrestrial kingdom." This answer—and I used to be guilty of this myself—reveals some confusion about what is really required of those who will inherit the celestial kingdom. Most unsettling, this line of terrestrial thinking demonstrates a possible misunderstanding about the fundamental role of Jesus Christ's Atonement and His divine ability to save God's children. The purposes of this book are to help clarify some of these doctrinal

---

*Subjects for this study were drawn from participants in three separate sessions of Especially for Youth (EFY) conferences. Youth ranged in age from fourteen to eighteen years old and were from different parts of the United States. Participants anonymously answered a written survey questionnaire that posed the question: "If you died and were judged today, what eternal kingdom do you think you would go to?" followed by three choices: celestial (top), terrestrial (middle), and telestial (bottom). It is interesting to note that fourteen youth (or 2 percent) of sampled participants handwrote "outer darkness" or "son of perdition" to indicate their eternal destiny, which was not even an option on the survey.

misunderstandings and to provide the hope we can all have for the celestial kingdom because of the Atonement of Jesus Christ.

The format of this book is a hypothetical gospel classroom with fictional students. However, most of the questions and comments come from real-life discussions with actual teenagers I have had as students over the years. I've included a profile page at the beginning of this book for each character to help the reader understand the varied backgrounds and perspectives of the students being represented. You may find that some of the characters, and some of their questions, reflect your own thinking and ideas or those of teenagers you know.

It is my sincere desire that through the discussion that follows in *I'm Not Perfect. Can I Still Go to Heaven?* we can all better understand what is truly required to inherit the celestial kingdom and find hope in the heart of the gospel that will take us there: the Atonement of Jesus Christ.

STUDENT PROFILES

David Young

Wall | **Info** | **Photos** | **Videos**

Basic Information

Nicknames:	Dave, Davey, King David, Nephi Jr.
Gender:	Male
Height:	5'11"
Birthday:	September 28
Religion:	The Church of Jesus Christ of Latter-day Saints

Describe yourself in 30 words or less:

Serious, motivated, kind, spiritual, musical, funny, smart, athletic, leader . . . all rolled into one.

Personal Information

Activities: I am pretty serious about my studies and enrolled in a lot of high school college credit courses, so I spend a lot of time doing home-work. I want to get into med school so I'm try-ing to get as far ahead as possible right now. I run cross-country in the fall and track in the spring. I sing tenor in the school choir dur-ing the winter and that keeps me busy. I play the cello. I am also into swing and ballroom dancing. I love fly-fish-ing, camping, and hik-ing, and other activities with my Scout troop. I am the first assistant in my priests quorum. I like to spend time with my family.

Friends

Justin Owens | Dirk Otterson | Trevor (T.D.) Dawkins

Kathryn (Katie) Bennett | Lindsay Johnson | Mikayla Nelson

Olivia Collins

Favorite books:	Church books such as the Book of Mormon, *Jesus the Christ, Mormon Doctrine*. But I also like classic series books such as *The Lord of the Rings, The Chronicles of Narnia,* and the Harry Potter novels.
Favorite music genre:	'50s, classical, instrumental, ballroom music, EFY CDs
Who you'd like to meet:	Joseph Smith, George Washington. And I'd love to see Yo-Yo Ma in concert.
Goal you'd like to achieve this year:	Get my mission papers ready and receive my mission call.
Favorite phrase:	"I will go and do the things which the Lord hath commanded" (1 Nephi 3:7).

Contact Information

E-mail:	davidjr@youngfamily.book

Job Information

Description:	I bag groceries, stack produce, and load bags into cars for old ladies at the local market.

Dirk Otterson

Wall | **Info** | **Photos** | **Videos**

Basic Information

Nicknames:	People pretty much just call me Dirk.
Gender:	Male
Height:	6'1"
Birthday:	January 27
Religion:	I'm LDS. My mom and dad aren't really active in the Mormon Church, and sometimes I miss, too, but I'm a pretty good hombre overall, ya know? Lots of love for Jesus and stuff. I have a brother serving a mission right now, and he worries about me and tries to keep me on the straight and narrow. He doesn't think my boardin' friends are the best influence on me.

Personal Information

Activities:	I've got mad skills at hanging out with my friends. I am also on the brink of being a professional TV watcher. I rock the bass guitar in a band with my buddies (our band name is Unusable Signal if you want to check us on the Web). Snowboarding and skating are my two loves.

Describe yourself in 30 words or less:

I am a skateboarding, snowboard-riding bro with floppy hair, Vans, and am usually sporting a sweet ol' beanie. I love worn old T-shirts, backside 720s, and my music.

Friends

David Young

Justin Owens

Trevor (T.D.) Dawkins

Kathryn (Katie) Bennett

Lindsay Johnson

Mikayla Nelson

Olivia Collins

Favorite books:	Books? What are books? I learn from life more than I learn from literature.
Favorite music genre:	Anything alternative, some punk, and a little Indie rock n' roll always do the trick for me.
Who you'd like to meet:	Shaun White, Tony Hawk, Ghandi, Joseph Smith, and the person who invented ice cream.
Goal you'd like to achieve this year:	Achieving nirvana.
Favorite phrase:	Dude, it's gotta be "dude."

Contact Information

E-mail:	dirk_360@snowboarder.book

Job Information

Description:	I am a master taco maker with my bros at Taco Grande's.

Justin Owens

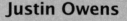

| Wall | **Info** | Photos | Videos |

Basic Information

Nicknames:	I don't really like my name, so my friends call me J. O. because of my initials.
Gender:	Male
Height:	5'7"
Birthday:	May 15
Religion:	LDS . . . If I wasn't, my mom would probably disown me.

Describe yourself in 30 words or less:

Let's put it this way: you would never see me on the cover of a health or sports magazine. (I'm not really into sports. Not that I really want to be around athlete guys anyway.)

Personal Information

Activities:	If it has a TV or computer attached to it, I like it. I'm also into computer programming and graphic and Web design. (I've already created a few of my own video games.)
Favorite books:	Whatever is NOT assigned as homework.
Favorite music genre:	Industrial and rock.
Who you'd like to meet:	Bill Gates, Steve Jobs
Goal you'd like to achieve this year:	Not failing my creative writing class.
Favorite phrase:	"You won't like me when I'm angry . . ."

Friends

 David Young

 Dirk Otterson

 Trevor (T.D.) Dawkins

 Kathryn (Katie) Bennett

 Lindsay Johnson

 Mikayla Nelson

 Olivia Collins

Contact Information

E-mail: justin3481908@video
gamers.book

Job Information

Description: I work at Music Exchange
where you can swap your
old CDs/DVDs/video
games for cash.

Trevor (T. D.) Dawkins

Wall | **Info** | **Photos** | **Videos**

Basic Information

Nicknames:	T. D., Trev, T-Dawg, Trey
Gender:	Male
Height:	6'3½"
Birthday:	November 10
Religion:	LDS

Describe yourself in 30 words or less:

Ladies, just picture your ideal man and you got him.

Personal Information

Activities:	Football is the love of my life. I play middle linebacker and am one of the team captains. Nothing gets me more excited than to blind-side somebody. I also love to hunt and fish any chance I can get on the weekends. Working on old cars and trucks is also one of my hobbies. Me and my dad are restoring an old '69 Mustang Mach 1 and putting a 351 V8 into it. I love anything with engines. I snowmobile in the winter and do a lot of four-wheeling and boating in the summer.
Favorite books:	*Sports Illustrated & Outdoors Magazine*
Favorite music genre:	Is there any other real music than country music?

Friends

 David Young

 Dirk Otterson

 Justin Owens

 Kathryn (Katie) Bennett

 Lindsay Johnson

 Mikayla Nelson

 Olivia Collins

Who you'd like to meet:	Ray Lewis, Lawrence Taylor, Peyton Manning, Dale Earnhart.
Goal you'd like to achieve this year:	Bench 275 pounds.
Favorite phrase:	"No guts, no glory."

Contact Information

E-mail:	TDendzone@futureNFL.book

Job Information

Description:	In the summer I do landscaping and do snowplowing in the winter.

Kathryn (Katie) Bennett

Wall **Info** Photos Videos

Basic Information

Nicknames:	Kat, La Gata, K. T.
Gender:	Female
Height:	5'5"
Birthday:	October 16
Religion:	I am a member of The Church of Jesus Christ of Latter-day Saints (Mormon). However, I am open to and respectful of all other belief systems and ideas that promote inner happiness and community peace.

Describe yourself in 30 words or less:

I am still finding myself, so I find it difficult to describe myself. . . . The more I learn the less I know.

Personal Information

Activities:	I'm totally involved with anything that has to do with social issues and human rights. I'm really into philosophy lately—Kant, Locke, Marx. I love to write—especially poetry. I enjoy anything that has to do with the outdoors and nature: camping, hiking, rock climbing. I am a student body officer at my school, a member of the literary club, on the debate team, a member of the Future Business Leaders of America. I really want to make the world a better place.

Friends

Justin Owens

Dirk Otterson

Trevor (T.D.) Dawkins

David Young

Lindsay Johnson

Mikayla Nelson

Olivia Collins

Favorite books:	*The Grapes of Wrath, The Odyssey, Walden, Critique of Practical Reason, Civil Disobedience.*
Favorite music genre:	Alternative underground mainly, but I also like a little bluegrass, folk, jazz, soul, R&B, and even some classical music, depending on my mood.
Who you'd like to meet:	Martin Luther King Jr.
Goal you'd like to achieve this year:	Get accepted to Harvard, Yale, or Stanford.
Favorite phrase:	"Go green."

Contact Information

E-mail:	Katie@coexist.book

Job Information

Description:	I don't really have a job. My parents tell me that school and community involvement are my work. But I just returned from a summer of aid work in South America. I worked for a month in Peru at an orphanage and then for another month in Bolivia, giving vaccines to the Andean Indians.

Lindsay Johnson

Wall | **Info** | **Photos** | **Videos**

Basic Information

Nicknames:	Lynz, Z, Li'l Lin
Gender:	Female
Height:	5'9"
Birthday:	September 3
Religion:	LDS

Describe yourself in 30 words or less:

I should be on *American Idol.*

Personal Information

Activities:	Listening to music. Chillin' with my friends. Being with my family, especially my grand-parents and nieces and nephews. I play all kinds of sports. I'm on the school volleyball and basketball teams and run the 50, 100, and 400 in track. I like to watercolor paint in my free time. I love to sing and am in a cultural dance group, too.
Favorite books:	Whatever Oprah or my older sister likes.
Favorite music genre:	R&B, soul, rap, reggae.
Who you'd like to meet:	Oprah, any Olympic gold medalist, Georgia O'Keefe, Will Smith.
Goal you'd like to achieve this year:	Be on the all-state basketball team. Get accepted to nursing school.

Friends

David Young

Dirk Otterson

Trevor (T.D.) Dawkins

Kathryn (Katie) Bennett

Justin Owens

Mikayla Nelson

Olivia Collins

Favorite phrase: "'Sup?"

Contact Information

E-mail: Lynz@yougogirl.book

Job Information

Description: Fast food.

Mikayla Nelson

Wall | **Info** | **Photos** | **Videos**

Basic Information

Nicknames:	Micki, Kayla, La-la, "Like"-ayla.
Gender:	Female
Height:	5'3"
Birthday:	March 29
Religion:	Mormon

Describe yourself in 30 words or less:

I am a girl who just loves life and wants to make friends and help everyone be happy!

Personal Information

Activities:	I love dancing, tumbling, and gymnastics! I enjoy playing board games, going to parties, and hanging out with my teammates! I love going shopping and having new clothes! I love anything that is out in the sun! Oh, and did I mention, I like boys!?!?!?
Favorite books:	Anything with a good love story.
Favorite music genre:	I have no idea, there are so many! Really anything with a good beat that I can dance to!
Who you'd like to meet:	I really admire people like Mary Lou Retton.
Goal you'd like to achieve this year:	I want to go to beauty school to be a cosmetologist.

Friends

 David Young

 Dirk Otterson

 Justin Owens

 Kathryn (Katie) Bennett

 Lindsay Johnson

 Trevor (T.D.) Dawkins

 Olivia Collins

Favorite phrase:	I don't think I really have one. But my favorite saying is, "Life is too short to be anything but happy."

Contact Information

E-mail:	textgirl01@gotspirit.book

Job Information

Description:	I coach at cheer camps and teach dance.

Olivia Collins

Wall **Info** **Photos** **Videos**

Basic Information

Nicknames:	Livvy
Gender:	Female
Height:	5'5"
Birthday:	May 30
Religion:	I just converted to the LDS (Mormon) Church last year.

Describe yourself in 30 words or less:

I'm a quiet girl who likes kids, books, and helping people.

Personal Information

Activities:	I like to scrapbook and keep a journal. I go to the local elementary school three times a week and read books to kids in the after-school program. I like to knit and crochet. I just got a new camera and have started getting into photography.
Favorite books:	*Little Women* and anything from Jane Austen (especially *Pride and Prejudice*).
Favorite music genre:	Top 40 songs.
Who you'd like to meet:	Jane Austen, Laura Ingalls Wilder, Louisa May Alcott, Maria Montessori, Dr. Seuss.
Goal you'd like to achieve this year:	Find some friends at my new school. Be on the school newspaper staff.

Friends

David Young

Dirk Otterson

Trevor (T.D.) Dawkins

Kathryn (Katie) Bennett

Lindsay Johnson

Mikayla Nelson

Justin Owens

Favorite phrase:	"If you can read this, thank a teacher."

Contact Information

E-mail:	O_Collins@englishtutor.book

Job Information

Description:	I tutor other students.

CLASS #1

The Question and the Quandary

Thank you so much for being here in class today. I hope you get something from the next few lessons and feel edified. Let's jump right into it with a hypothetical question: Imagine for a moment, as the prophet Alma said to his people, that you "were called to die at this time" (Alma 5:27) and were required "to stand before God to be judged according to the deeds which have been done in the mortal body" (Alma 5:15). Here is what I want to know: If you died and were to be judged today, which eternal kingdom do you think you would go to?

> The celestial kingdom (the top)
> The terrestrial kingdom (the middle)
> The telestial kingdom (the bottom)

If you could please anonymously write down your answer on a piece of paper and pass it forward to me, I'm interested to see what your answers are.

I have asked this question to hundreds of youth across America, and the answers are usually similar. Looking at the responses from our class, we fall right into roughly the same pattern as well. Here is how our class broke out:

52% of you think you will make it to the celestial kingdom.

40% of you think you are going to go to the terrestrial kingdom.

5% of you think you are going to the bottom kingdom, the telestial glory.

And one of you thought he or she is going to go to outer darkness with the sons of perdition. That wasn't even an option!

1

Dirk: Well, I heard that outer darkness is where you go if you have a prompting from the Holy Ghost and don't follow it. It's called like, denying the Holy Ghost or something, I think. So I'll 'fess up: that person was me. Sorry, dude, but I put it down because there are times when I know I should do something and I don't do it. You know, I get a prompting and don't follow it.

Thanks for 'fessing up, Dirk, but I think you might be being a little harsh on yourself. You are right in that the sin against the Holy Ghost is an unforgivable sin (see Alma 39:5–6); but not following a personal prompting from the Spirit is much different than the sin against the Holy Ghost that makes you a son of perdition.

 Olivia: Well, so what do you have to do to sin against the Holy Ghost and go to outer darkness then?

The Prophet Joseph Smith answered that question. He said: "What must a man do to commit the unpardonable sin? He must receive the Holy Ghost, have the heavens opened unto him, and know God, and then sin against Him. . . . He has got to say that the sun does not shine while he sees it; he has got to deny Jesus Christ when the heavens have been opened unto him, and to deny the plan of salvation with his eyes open to the truth of it."[1] President Spencer W. Kimball taught that "the sin against the Holy Ghost requires such knowledge that it is manifestly impossible for the [average member of the Church] to commit such a sin."[2] In other words, it isn't a punishment that anyone in this class needs to worry will happen to them right now because it is nearly impossible for ordinary Church members such as us to commit that kind of sin.

 Dirk: I'm suddenly feeling much better now. Thanks, bro.

I'm glad that helped. Thank the Prophet Joseph Smith and

President Kimball for clarifying that for us. Now let's get back to the poll about which kingdom you feel you will go to: as a class, your overall answers reveal an unsettling phenomenon and mindset among many of the youth of the Church, and many adults for that matter. I would assume that almost all of you in this class go to church pretty much every week. You serve in the priesthood and in class presidencies and callings. You probably attend Young Men and Young Women fairly often. Most of you are enrolled in seminary. I bet some of you even spend your summers paying to go to gospel-oriented camps like EFY, right? So what I want to know is why roughly 50 percent of you—a group of youth who are striving and struggling to do what is right and who are active in the Church—don't think you are going to make it to the celestial kingdom? If you aren't going to make it to heaven, then who will?

 Olivia: Well, people like the prophets and apostles and other good Church leaders, I think.

I'll agree with you on that one, Olivia. If anyone is going to make it, it will be the Lord's prophets and apostles. So there are a few hundred people out of a few billion. Not very good odds. Anyone else going to make it?

 David: Little kids who have died before the age of eight. They are guaranteed, right?

Good, Dave, you're right on with that one as well. Joseph Smith, in a vision of the celestial kingdom, said that all children who die before they are eight years old will automatically be saved in the celestial kingdom (see D&C 137:10). But, still, if you don't fit into that small minority of God's children who are prophets or unaccountable children who have passed away, it almost appears near hopeless. None of us in this room fits into either of those two categories.

 Justin: Not yet. David probably will fit into the "prophet"

category soon, though. He's like a modern-day Nephi. So he might make it.

So prophets, young children, and David will go to heaven. At least we think one of us in here might squeeze in! Why do others of you think you won't make it?

Mikayla: I'll be brave and speak up. I wrote down that I thought I would go to the terrestrial kingdom. The reason that I put that is because I've made some mistakes in my life, so I don't think I'm really worthy of the celestial kingdom. At the same time, I'm not like a murderer or anything, so I don't think I'll go to the telestial kingdom.

Dirk: That's kind of the way I was thinking, too. It's, like, the celestial kingdom is perfect and pure and holy, and I'm just not that. But the bottom kingdom is for, like, real bad sinners, you know? Rapists and adulterers and stuff, and I'm not like that, either. So I just thought, hey, glad God made a middle kingdom for dudes like me!

Thanks for your thoughts, you guys. Your answers are very enlightening, and I suspect that your reasoning is similar to most others in the class who feel that they aren't going to make it to the celestial kingdom. Most of us use similar logic when it comes to the kingdoms of glory. We think: Well, I still make mistakes and I'm far from perfect, so I won't go to the celestial kingdom. But I'm not a horrible person, so I won't go to the telestial kingdom, either—looks like it's the middle of the road in the terrestrial kingdom for me!

Katie: But isn't that kind of what the scriptures teach? I've read and heard lots of verses that say things like, "Heaven is spotless, so if you are guilty of any sin you can't go there, or it won't be spotless anymore," or something like that.

Yes, there are a lot of verses like that in the scriptures. Nephi is the one who taught that. Let's take a look at a few scriptures that are similar to the ones Katie is referring to. Katie, will you read 1 Nephi 15:33–34?

Katie: Sure. It says: "If their works have been filthiness they must needs be filthy; and if they be filthy it must needs be that they cannot dwell in the kingdom of God; if so, the kingdom of God must be filthy also. But behold, I say unto you, the kingdom of God is not filthy, and there cannot any unclean thing enter into the kingdom of God; wherefore there must needs be a place of filthiness prepared for that which is filthy."

David: Here is another one in Alma 11:37. It says, "And I say unto you again that [God] cannot save [us] in [our] sins; for I cannot deny his word, and he hath said that no unclean thing can inherit the kingdom of heaven. . . . Therefore, ye cannot be saved in your sins."

And just to top it off, let me add this one where the Apostle Paul teaches us that "all have sinned, and come short of the glory of God" (Romans 3:23). Thanks, Paul, for that little pick-me-up! We all feel much better now. The logic, then, is this: we all sin, and our sins make us filthy, and the kingdom of God—the celestial kingdom—cannot have anything filthy in it or else it will become filthy, so there must be another place that filthy people like us who have made mistakes go, right?

Katie: But everyone has sinned. Isn't that why we have repentance, so we can be forgiven of those sins?

Yes, it is. But even though we may have repented of some of our sins, does that mean we have repented of *all* of our sins? Are there other sins and shortcomings we are carrying that we haven't overcome yet that are making us imperfect, even if we are repenting of others? If

5

somehow we do repent of *all* our sins and become perfectly clean, how long does it take before we sin again, and once again are filthy, even in the least bit?

 Justin: About 1.5 milliseconds for me.

So what are the odds that when we die, we will be in a perfect state of sinlessness?

 Trevor: C'mon . . . now you're depressing us. I thought you said this lesson was going to uplift us and help us. After what you just taught us I think that the 50 percent in the class who thought they were going to the celestial kingdom should change their vote. You're worse than Paul and his "pick-me-up."

Oh, Trevor, I haven't even shared the most depressing verse yet. This is the scripture that usually causes most of our celestial discouragement. Go to Matthew 5:48. What does Jesus say? "Be ye therefore perfect, even as your Father which is in heaven is perfect." This verse poses a serious dilemma: God wants us to be perfect—perfectly clean, perfectly obedient, and perfectly worthy. But other than Jesus, none of us is perfect. Since we all live in a state of sinfulness to one degree or another and therefore fall short of perfection, the majority of us don't think we will make it to the celestial kingdom.

 Mikayla: Well, it looks like maybe we were right in thinking that only the prophet and little kids will go to heaven. Who else will make it, then?

You sound just like Jesus' disciples when the Savior told a rich young man—who was doing all he could to keep the commandments—that he still lacked the qualities of perfection (see Matthew 19:16–24). After this encounter, the scriptures say: "When his disciples heard it, they were exceedingly amazed, saying, Who then can be saved?" (Matthew 19:25). Sound familiar?

 Katie: Well, then, I'm serious—who really can be saved? It's frustrating.

Listen to what the Savior says in the next verse of the story, and we'll pick up there in our next class: "But Jesus beheld them, and said unto them, With men this is impossible; but with God all things are possible" (Matthew 19:26).

CLASS #2

Understanding "Perfection"

If I were to ask you which of all the Lord's commandments is the hardest to keep, which one would you say?

 Lindsay: I think really being honest is the most difficult. It's hard to be one hundred percent honest in everything we do, like in school and with our teachers and stuff.

 Trevor: Probably the one where it tells us we need to watch and control our thoughts. That's pretty hard to do all the time, especially as a teenager.

 Olivia: Well, for teenagers, maybe it's honoring our father and mother. Especially when they might be wrong or do things you don't agree with that hurt your family.

 Justin: What about "thou shalt not kill"? I think most kids struggle with that one . . . Relax, I'm just kiddin'.

 Trevor: Too many shoot-'em-up video games lately, Justin?

Those all are difficult commandments to keep, and, for some, maybe the commandment not to kill is the most difficult one for them. But you haven't mentioned the one I thought you might, especially given what we've been talking about.

 David: Loving the Lord with all our heart?

8

No.

 Katie: Loving our neighbor as ourselves?

Not that one, either. Although, by all means, please do that.

 Mikayla: Keeping the law of chastity or the Word of Wisdom?

Strike three. Let's read what Elder Russell M. Nelson of the Quorum of the Twelve said is the hardest: "If I were to ask which of the Lord's commandments is most difficult to keep, many of us might cite Matthew 5:48: 'Be ye therefore perfect, even as your Father which is in heaven is perfect.'"[1]

 Katie: I didn't think that being perfect was a commandment. I thought it was more like a goal or something that we should try to do, but not written in stone.

Nope, it's a commandment, sister. Actually, striving to keep all the other commandments leads up to fulfilling this ultimate commandment—to be perfect.

 David: But we just talked about the fact that none of us is perfect. So can we really keep that commandment?

Well, let's read the rest of Elder Nelson's quote to see what he says about that. David, go ahead and read, if you will.

 David: "Keeping this commandment can be a concern because each of us is far from perfect, both spiritually and temporally. . . .
"When comparing one's personal performance with the supreme standard of the Lord's expectation, the reality of imperfection can at times be depressing. . . .

"We all need to remember: men are that they might have joy—not guilt trips! We also need to remember that the Lord gives no commandments that are impossible to obey. *But sometimes we fail to comprehend them fully.*"[2]

Notice what Elder Nelson said: God never gives us commandments we can't keep, so if we feel as though it is an impossible commandment to be perfect, then maybe we just don't understand something about what God is asking of us. Maybe our misunderstanding is that we think that *we* need to be perfect in order to go to the celestial kingdom.

 David: I've struggled with this a lot in my life, because even though I know I am far from perfect, I still expect myself to be. My whole life I have tried to do what is right and to be as good as possible. One of my friends' mom even started calling me Nephi Jr. when I was young because she thought I never did anything wrong. And because my dad is the stake president I feel like other people expect me to be a perfect member of the Church too—that I can't ever make any mistakes. Last year when our school choir went on an out-of-state performance tour, a few parents came with us as chaperones, and one of them was from my stake. On the last night before we came home some of my friends and I played a fairly harmless prank. But when we got caught, I was the only one who got in trouble by the chaperone because he said he didn't expect I would ever do something questionable like that. It just frustrates me sometimes to be held to a standard—by myself, my neighbors, and the Lord—that seems impossible.

That can be frustrating, David. Just so you know, there are a lot of people out there similar to you—young and old, male and female—who are amazing people but who hold themselves to such a high standard of perfection that they never really feel as though they are doing well enough. In other people's eyes they might appear exemplary, but inside they feel as though they are always falling a little short, a little under the bar they have set for themselves. But take a look at footnote *b* for Matthew 5:48. What does the word *perfection* really imply in the Greek translation for this commandment to be "perfect," since Greek was one of the original languages of the New Testament?

 David: The "GR" thing, right? It says "complete, finished, fully developed."

Good. So let's rephrase the verse based on that translation: "Be ye therefore complete, finished, or fully developed." When we change the language of the scripture, using these words, what new meanings might it imply?

 Katie: It seems to imply that perfection is a more of a process. That it is something that doesn't happen immediately.

Now we are getting somewhere! Great insight, Katie. Elder Nelson explained that the word for "perfect" in Matthew 5:48 derives from the Greek word *teleios*. He said:

"Please note that the word does not imply 'freedom from error'; it implies 'achieving a distant objective.' . . .

"*Teleios* is not a total stranger to us. From it comes the prefix *tele-* that we use every day. *Telephone* literally means 'distant talk.' *Television* means 'to see distantly.' *Telephoto* means 'distant light,' and so on."[3]

Understanding that the commandment to be perfect is not something that will be achieved for a long time should relieve us of a little immediate stress. As a matter of fact, this commandment to be perfect can't be fulfilled in this lifetime. It is a doctrinal impossibility. Let me say that again: The commandment to be perfect can't be fulfilled in this lifetime. It is a doctrinal impossibility.[4]

 Trevor: You mean you can't keep the commandment to be

perfect in this life? How would we keep that commandment, then?

Well, as we just learned, being perfect—or fully developed—is a distant achievement. So distant, as a matter of fact, that it is beyond mortality. Let me show you what I mean by asking you a question: Was Jesus perfect?

 Trevor: Of course He was. He was the only sinless person to ever live.

Good, Trevor, you are right. I testify that Jesus was completely spotless and lived a life free from sin. But remember, Elder Nelson just taught us that the commandment in Matthew to "be ye therefore perfect" doesn't have to do with sin. It has to do with accomplishing a distant objective; an objective that not even Jesus accomplished in His mortal life.

 Trevor: I still don't get it.

Well, when Jesus commanded us to be perfect, who did He compare the idea of perfection to in Matthew 5:48?

 Trevor: Let me reread it. It says, "Be ye therefore perfect, even as your Father which is in heaven is perfect." So he compares perfection to Heavenly Father.

Yes. Exactly. But don't you guys find it interesting, that our Savior likened perfection to Heavenly Father, and not to Himself? After all, Jesus was sinless! If that isn't "perfect," what was He referring to?

 Olivia: Maybe He was just being humble. So, He didn't want to put himself in there, even though He was sinless.

That's a good idea, because Jesus was also the most humble person ever to walk this earth, but I think we can learn something more than humility from this statement—I think He was trying to teach us something about perfection. I say that because of what Jesus taught after His Resurrection when He appeared to the Nephites. Open up your Book of Mormon to 3 Nephi 12:48. Justin, will you read that for us?

Justin: "Therefore I would that ye should be perfect even as I, or your Father who is in heaven is perfect."

Justin, what do you see is the main difference between this verse in the Book of Mormon, as compared to the same verse given in the Bible?

Justin: I guess that Jesus added Himself in there now as someone who is perfect.

Right on, Justin. Notice that to the Nephites, Jesus says, "Be perfect *even as I*, or your Father who is in heaven" (3 Nephi 12:48; emphasis added). Why would He add Himself as a perfect being now, along with His Father, but didn't when He gave the same teaching to his disciples in Jerusalem?

Lindsay: Maybe it was in the Bible originally, but it was taken out over the years, and since the Book of Mormon is more accurate, it was put in there.

That is a great insight about the Book of Mormon and the translation of the Bible, but Joseph Smith didn't add Jesus' perfection into Matthew 5:48 when he did his inspired translation of the Bible.

Dirk: Maybe he just forgot to say it in Jerusalem. Slipped His mind, ya know?

Mikayla: Well, is it because when He was talking to His disciples in Jerusalem, He wasn't resurrected yet, but when He appeared to the Nephites, He was resurrected?

Exactly!

 Dirk: I suddenly feel much less perfect than Mikayla.

Elder Russell M. Nelson said: "That Jesus attained eternal perfection *following* his resurrection is confirmed in the Book of Mormon. . . . This time he listed himself along with his Father as a perfected personage. Previously, he had not.

"Resurrection is a requisite for eternal perfection."[5]

Jesus himself taught this truth—that we need to be resurrected in order to be perfected—to His New Testament apostles when He said, on "the third day I *shall* be perfected" (Luke 13:32; emphasis added).

 Mikayla: Oh, like His third day in the tomb, right?

Right. Notice that Jesus was saying His perfection, or His being complete, was a future event for even Him after His mortal life was completed. He couldn't be "fully developed" or "complete" until He had become like God the Father. And since God the Father has an immortal body of flesh and bones (see D&C 130:22), Jesus couldn't say He was complete and perfect until He had attained His resurrected, immortal body as well. And neither can we.

 Katie: Well, what you're saying, then, is that the commandment to be perfect not only can't be achieved in this life, but that we can't achieve it by ourselves, either.

What do you mean we can't achieve it by ourselves?

Katie: Just that. If real perfection requires resurrection, we can't resurrect ourselves, can we? We have to be resurrected by Jesus. So what I'm saying is that we shouldn't think that we have to attain perfection on our own.

Katie, that is a great insight. As a matter of fact, in light of what Katie just taught us, let's take a look at footnote *b* for Matthew 5:48, the footnote that takes you to D&C 67:13. Flip there quickly please and let's read it.

 Lindsay: It says, "Continue in patience until ye are perfected."

So what do you get out of that, Lindsay? Why do I say that verse is interesting, given what Katie just said about not being able to fulfill the commandment to be perfect on our own?

 Lindsay: Well, this verse makes it seem like perfection is something that will happen to us. It doesn't say we should be perfect, but that we should continue on until we are perfected. Almost like perfection is something that will happen to us because of something else, not something that we will do ourselves.

And what, or *who,* will perfect us?

 Lindsay: Well, if we have to be resurrected to be perfect, then what will make us perfected is the Atonement. Jesus is the one who will perfect us.

Excellent! When we more fully understand what is meant by "be ye therefore perfect," then, it gives us hope. The two main points to understand the commandment to be perfect are these: (1) Perfection is something that cannot be accomplished in mortality because it requires a resurrected body. The concepts of mortality and perfection are incompatible. (2) Because perfection requires resurrection, perfection is not something we do; it is something that will be done to us. We cannot accomplish it by ourselves. Let's not think that *we* need to be perfect, meaning flawless and sinless in this life, in order to be perfected and make it to the celestial kingdom. Elder Bruce R. McConkie said, "[You] don't need to get a complex or get a feeling that you have to be perfect to be saved. *You* don't."[6] Elder Nelson summed it up this way: "We need not be dismayed if our earnest efforts toward perfection now seem so arduous and endless. Perfection is pending. It can come in full only after the Resurrection and only through the Lord."[7] The fact that perfection is not something that we can accomplish in this life, nor is it something that we can accomplish ourselves, should ease the burden of perfection off our mortal shoulders and onto the immortal and capable shoulders of Jesus, allowing us to lift our heads up in hope. If we really understand that *we,* on our own, never were expected to be perfect in this life, then suddenly the doors to the celestial kingdom should seem more open to us.

 Katie: So if we don't have to be perfect, what is expected of us to make it to heaven? What do we have to do, then?

It depends on what you mean when you say "make it to heaven." There are actually three different "heavens."

 Katie: Are you talking about the three different degrees of glory? Like the celestial, terrestrial, and telestial kingdoms?

That is exactly what I'm talking about. Let's make sure we understand the true idea of "heaven" first, and then we can start to look at the requirements for each kingdom. I can tell you this much up front: perfection as we usually think of it *is not required of us* to make it into any of them . . . even into the celestial kingdom.

CLASS #3

Heaven, Hell, and Degrees of Glory

How many of you have begun looking into what is required to be accepted for a college? Katie, I bet you have.

 Katie: Yeah, I have.

Where do you want to go?

 Katie: I'm thinking any of the Ivy League schools, if they'll let me in. It's pretty tough to crack, though.

What are some of the requirements to get in?

 Katie: Well, you have to have a high SAT or ACT score, and be among the top in your graduating class . . .

 Justin: And have lots of money like Katie's family . . .

 Katie: Anyway, you have to be really involved in extra-curricular activities. Like, I'm a student body officer, and in FBLA, and I'm the editor of the yearbook. Service in the community helps, too. I went to Peru this last summer to help with an orphanage down there for about a month, partly because I wanted to do the service, but part of it—and I hate to say it but I will—is that it looks good on the application. The schools look at all that stuff, and I know it.

That's pretty cool that you have done all that, and I hope you're able to get into a good school because of it. I'm interested in your comment that you know what the schools look at and what is required to get in. That obviously helps shape your goals and your behavior, I would guess. Who else is looking into the requirements, and where do you want to go?

Olivia: I want to be an elementary school teacher, so I plan on just going close by here to the university. They have a good teaching program, and it's a little easier and less expensive to get into, especially because I'll probably be paying for it myself.

So you already know not only what you need to get in, but how much it will cost as well?

Olivia: Yeah. It's pretty expensive for me, but I think I can do it by working and saving.

Dirk: I know what's expected to get into the school I want to go to.

Yeah? Where do you want to go?

Dirk: To the community college. I think the only requirement to get in there is to have a high-school diploma and to be breathing. I'm pretty good at the breathing thing—maybe I could even major in it. I'm shootin' for the stars, ya know?

Always aiming high, Dirk. I love it. Well, thanks for sharing that info. I bring up entrance to colleges because getting into college has a lot of parallels to getting into heaven. Can you think of some?

Lindsay: Well, there are different types of colleges—different levels. You know, like we were saying, there are Ivy League, average universities, and community colleges. Same in the next life. There are different levels of heaven. Different degrees, ya know?

Good comparison. What else?

Mikayla: You need to know what is required to get into those schools if you want to qualify for them and get accepted. If you know what they are looking for, you can try to measure up to that in high school. You'll know what schools are within your reach and which ones are, like, just in your dreams.

Great insight as well. But what if you don't *really* know the acceptance standards of a school? What if you just assume that the acceptance standards are way out of your league? Like Mikayla, why don't you apply for an Ivy League school? You're smart and capable and involved.

Mikayla: Oh, thanks. But I don't think they'd accept me. You know, cheerleading versus orphaned children in Peru . . . I don't think I quite measure up.

Are you sure? Or are you just cutting yourself out of the possibility without really knowing what is required, by just *assuming* you don't measure up? Have you really looked into it?

Mikayla: No, I haven't really. I just thought it would be a waste of time. But I honestly don't really know what the standards are to get into an Ivy League school.

I think a lot of us do the same with the celestial kingdom: we assume the standard of entrance is so beyond our ability to enter that we give up before really ever knowing what the entrance standards are.

So if we are comparing getting into college with getting into heaven, then where can we find the acceptance requirements for heaven written down?

 David: Well, in the scriptures. The answers are always in the scriptures.

Anywhere in particular?

 David: I think section 76 of the Doctrine and Covenants is the main one on the three degrees of glory, right?

Right. Actually, section 76 is going to be our primary text of study for the next few classes. It is an amazing section. Part of what makes it so incredible is that it spells out specifically what the requirements are for entrance into each of the three eternal kingdoms. The eternal "acceptance standards," so to speak—so we can really know if we qualify or not. Speaking of section 76, President Wilford Woodruff said, "Any man may know through [Doctrine and Covenants section 76] what his part and condition will be [in eternity]."[1]

 Olivia: Before we go on, can I ask a question?

Of course.

 Olivia: Sorry, this might be a dumb question. But since I've only been a member of the Church for a few years, I don't know a lot about the whole concept of different heavens. I was raised as a mainstream Christian, and all we ever talked about in the next life was heaven and hell. So I'm a little confused when we talk about three heavens. Do we believe in heaven and hell? Or what is hell, then?

That is not a dumb question; it is a great one. For me, there are many things that testify to the truthfulness of the restored gospel of Jesus Christ. One of those is the doctrine of three kingdoms of glory. Before Joseph Smith reopened our understanding on this topic, the world was consigned to think of merely heaven and hell, like you said. One place—heaven—is pure and holy and full of angels and harps and clouds. The other—hell—is full of flames and fire and brimstone and weeping and wailing and gnashing of teeth.

 Katie: Well, don't the scriptures tell us the idea of simply two places, a heaven and a hell? Isn't that where we get all the weeping and wailing stuff from, anyway?

Yes, the scriptures do say that. But Joseph Smith helped us understand that where we go after we die is not where we go for eternity. Just like the rest of the Christian world, we believe that when we die there are two primary divisions, a heaven and a hell, so to speak. But in the restored Church, we call them different names. Anyone want to venture what I am talking about?

 Olivia: Are you talking about the spirit world?

Yes, I am. And what do we call "heaven" and "hell" in the spirit world?

 David: Spirit paradise and spirit prison.

Exactly. The Book of Mormon prophet Alma teaches us that there is a "state of the soul between death and the resurrection" where the righteous go to paradise, or heaven, and the wicked go to prison, or hell (see Alma 40:11–14). And that "thus [the wicked] remain in this state, as well as the righteous in paradise, until the time of their resurrection" (vs. 14).

Now, if this were the end of our doctrine on the next life, we wouldn't be much different from the rest of Christianity on the subject. But notice Alma's last statement, that we will be in paradise or prison "until the time of [our] resurrection." As Joseph Smith pondered the scriptures, he realized that it isn't just the *righteous* who will be resurrected. ALL who have lived will be. Let's mark a few of these verses that teach this important doctrine, that everyone ever born, the righteous *and the wicked,* will be resurrected. Go to 1 Corinthians 15:21–22. Lindsay, will you read?

Lindsay: "For since by man came death, by man came also the resurrection of the dead. For as in Adam all die, even so in Christ shall all be made alive."

Thank you. Notice that *all* will be made alive, or resurrected. Let's look at another one. Go to John 5:28–29. Trevor, will you read that one?

Trevor: "Marvel not at this: for the hour is coming, in the which all that are in the graves shall hear his voice, and shall come forth; they that have done good, unto the resurrection of life; and they that have done evil, unto the resurrection of damnation."

What doctrine do you notice regarding who will be resurrected in those verses?

Olivia: Like it says in Corinthians, all will be. Everyone who has ever been born.

Justin: So everyone will be resurrected? Good or bad? Even like Hitler and Stalin? That's awesome.

Sort of. It's awesome that Christ is so merciful and kind and good as to resurrect everyone, but part of the reason that Christ will resurrect everyone is so that all will be accountable to Him and stand to be judged by Him (see 2 Nephi 9:22). I'm not quite sure if Hitler will be feeling too awesome at that moment.

As Joseph Smith pondered on the truth that all will be resurrected, he concluded that "'if God rewarded every one according to the deeds done in the body, the term "Heaven," as intended for the Saints' eternal home, must include more kingdoms than one'" (D&C 76, section heading). The Lord then revealed to Joseph the doctrine of three kingdoms and degrees of resurrected glory, or three heavens. The cool thing is that although this doctrine of three degrees of glory seemed new and revolutionary to the majority of the Christian world, it is plainly taught in the New Testament. Most churches, blinded by the years of the Great Apostasy, apparently just missed it.

 Olivia: Where does the New Testament talk about having three degrees of glory?

Paul talks about being "caught up to the third heaven" in a vision in 2 Corinthians 12:2. Is it possible to be taken up into the third heaven if there isn't a first or a second heaven? And in his first recorded letter to the Corinthians, Paul taught about the celestial and terrestrial glories. Mark these in 1 Corinthians 15:40–42 if you haven't done so already—making sure you note the Joseph Smith translation on footnote *a* of 1 Corinthians 15:40:

"Also celestial bodies, and bodies terrestrial, and bodies telestial; but the glory of the celestial, one; and the terrestrial, another; and the telestial, another.

"There is one glory of the sun, and another glory of the moon, and another glory of the stars; for one star differeth from another star in glory.

"So also is the resurrection of the dead."

Amazing! Those verses regarding the degrees of glory have sat there for hundreds of years, being passed over or misunderstood, until the great Prophet of the Restoration came along and gave them meaning!

Trevor: Are those verses in the same Bibles that other Christians use?

The Joseph Smith Translation adds the word *telestial* to Paul's explanation, but aside from that, yes, they are, my friend.

 Trevor: Then why don't other people believe in three degrees of heaven in the resurrection?

I don't know, Trevor. I couldn't speak for them. Frankly, if you or I had never heard of the Church or if Joseph Smith and the Restoration had never happened, we probably would pass over those verses or interpret them incorrectly as well. We would probably believe merely in a heaven and hell just as most others do.

 Dirk: You gotta love Joseph.

Yes, Dirk, we do, indeed.

 Mikayla: The whole three degrees makes sense if you, like, think about it. Because there aren't just good and bad people on earth, ya know? There are righteous people who love and follow Jesus, and there are wicked people who do bad stuff, like murder and robbing and other violent crimes. But there are also a lot of people who don't fall into either group—people in the middle.

 Trevor: Yeah, kind of like athletes. There aren't just good and bad football players on our team. There are the stars and starters. Then there are those that get some playing time for a few plays here and there. Then there are others who almost never get off the bench.

When you think about it, the idea of three degrees of heaven makes good, logical sense: different places prepared for people according to their level of righteousness. What's amazing about this restored doctrine of everyone being resurrected—and that there are three divisions of heaven or kingdoms of glory—is the underlying truth that *God will save* all *His children in heaven* to one degree or another. All of God's children, except the sons of perdition, will receive a kingdom of glory—a kingdom of *heaven*. Even the telestial kingdom is a *heaven*.

 Justin: So the telestial kingdom is NOT full of flames and heat and people burning and wailing in it and stuff?

No, it isn't. Actually, the telestial kingdom is better than being on the best parts of this mortal earth. I'll show you why I say that in a minute when we study the qualities and conditions of that kingdom. For now, just know that *all* of God's children—except the sons of perdition—will be saved in a heaven, in a degree of *glory*. That is such a cool LDS doctrine—one that shows Christ's mercy and saving power, and God's love for all His children. Elder Quentin L. Cook of the Quorum of the Twelve Apostles summarized it this way: "Because of the Atonement of Jesus Christ, all spirits blessed by birth will ultimately be resurrected . . . and [excepting sons of perdition] inherit kingdoms of glory that are superior to our existence here on earth."[2] Truly the good Lord "saves *all* the works of his hands" (D&C 76:43; emphasis added). So let's look at what the Lord revealed through Joseph Smith in D&C 76 about who goes to which level of *heaven*: the heaven of the telestial, the heaven of the terrestrial, and the heaven of the celestial kingdoms.

CLASS #4

The Telestial Kingdom

Let's begin our study of the three heavens with the telestial—or lowest kingdom of glory—by reading D&C 76:81–86, 100–113. Read over those verses on your own and tell me what you find out about (a) the attributes or qualities of those who will inherit the telestial kingdom, and (b) what conditions will be like there.

All right, what did you find for (a) the attributes or qualities of those who will inherit the telestial kingdom?

David: Verse 82 says that the telestial kingdom is for those "who received not the gospel of Christ, neither the testimony of Jesus."

Good, David. What does that mean?

David: I assume it means they never joined the Church or accepted the gospel through baptism, even if they could have. Instead, they chose to reject the gospel. Is that right?

That's right. What else does it say about what types of people will go to the telestial kingdom?

Mikayla: It says in verse 103 that telestial people are the "liars, . . . and sorcerers, and adulterers, and whoremongers." I know what an adulterer is . . . but . . . what's a whoremonger?

26

A whoremonger is someone who sells or profits from immorality—like prostitution or, in our day, someone who produces and sells pornography could also be seen as a whoremonger. But the definition can also imply people who are promiscuous in their sexual activity outside of marriage. A whoremonger doesn't necessarily care if he or she is immoral or see anything wrong with it.

 Katie: Hold on one second. I can understand adulterers going to the bottom kingdom, because adultery breaks up families and marriages. But that's different than, you know, someone who isn't married messing around with their boyfriend and breaking the law of chastity, right?

Katie, that's a good question because the philosophy of the world says that immorality is really no big deal before you are married, especially if two people are in love. However, that rationalization is not true—*any* immorality is extremely serious in God's sight because it defiles the sacred power of procreation that God has given His children.[1] The scriptures call sex before marriage *fornication* and sex with someone other than your spouse after marriage *adultery*. Surely adultery is a more serious sin because it betrays the most sacred and solemn promises one makes in marriage and breaks up families, but both adultery *and* fornication are classified as immorality. Satan tries to deceive us by saying that sex before marriage isn't as big of a deal as adultery, so it's not all that bad. But we need to be wiser than that. Both fornication and adultery are sex outside of the marriage covenant, and both are a violation of the commandment of God to protect the sacred power that creates life. As a matter of fact, the Apostle Paul taught that not only adulterers miss out on going to the celestial kingdom, but fornicators do as well. Turn to 1 Corinthians 6:9–10. Katie, since you asked the question, will you read it?

 Katie: Sure. "Know ye not that the unrighteous shall not inherit the kingdom of God? Be not deceived: neither fornicators, nor idolaters, nor adulterers . . . shall inherit the kingdom of God."

Make sense?

 Katie: So, if I have this friend who has messed up and is sleeping with her boyfriend, she isn't going to go to the celestial kingdom?

That's what the scripture says. But here is the good news. Even those who have been immoral, though it is one of the most serious sins that can be committed, can be completely forgiven through repentance. Notice 1 Corinthians 6:11. Right after Paul says that immoral people won't go to heaven—what does he say to the Saints he was writing to?

 Katie: "And such were some of you: but ye are washed, but ye are sanctified, but ye are justified in the name of the Lord Jesus."

In other words, "Some of you saints in Corinth have been guilty of immorality. But now you've repented and changed your lives and have been baptized in the name of Christ, and His Atonement has cleansed and purified and covered you, so you are no longer guilty of that sin and can still go to heaven." *For the Strength of Youth* promises that those who are guilty of sexual immorality and repent can receive the Lord's forgiveness and have the full companionship of the Spirit with them again.[2]

 Katie: But if we keep being immoral and don't repent . . .

Then according to scripture, we won't make it. We simply cannot willfully rebel against God's command to be sexually pure, and abuse the divine power that God gave us to create life, and expect to go to the celestial kingdom.

Lindsay: I think you'd better go talk to your friend, girl.

Katie: I think you're right.

Sounds like a good idea. Okay, what else qualifies for the telestial kingdom?

Olivia: I've heard that murderers go to the telestial kingdom, but I don't see where it mentions murderers anywhere in section 76. Is the telestial kingdom where murderers will go?

The scriptures teach us two primary truths about the sin of murder: (1) For Latter-day Saints, it can be an unforgivable sin. D&C 42:18 says, "And now, behold, I speak unto the church. Thou shalt not kill; and he that kills shall not have forgiveness in this world, nor in the world to come." The Apostle John also tells us, "Ye know that no murderer hath eternal life abiding in him" (1 John 3:15). (2) Life is sacred, and because murder deprives an individual of time to experience all that God has in store for him, and the opportunity to repent as needed, murder is the worst sin someone can commit, next to denying the Holy Ghost. The prophet Alma taught this in Alma 39:5. Section 76 is silent on the eternal fate of murderers, but if adulterers go to the telestial kingdom, and murder is a worse sin than adultery, it is safe to assume that unrepentant murderers will also go to the telestial kingdom.[3]

So, thus far, we see that those who will go to the telestial kingdom are:

1. Those who reject the gospel in this life and the next;
2. Those who are guilty of immorality;
3. And those who are murderers.

Have we missed anything?

Justin: D&C 76:103 says that the telestial kingdom is also where liars go.

 Katie: But doesn't everyone lie a little, though? Is anyone perfectly honest? If all liars go to the telestial kingdom, it seems that we will all go there.

Good question, Katie. I think we all have lied at times in our life. But I'm not sure if that puts us on par with adulterers, murderers, and the like. Look at the end of D&C 76:103. It says that those who go to the telestial kingdom includes "whosoever *loves* and makes a lie" (emphasis added). I think there is a difference between *loving* outright dishonesty and what we might call "smaller" forms of dishonesty such as not telling the truth and then feeling guilt and remorse over it. Remember, those who *love* being dishonest usually end up committing other telestial sins connected to dishonesty, such as adultery, fraud, stealing, and so on.

 Katie: That makes sense.

 Dirk: It bugs me when people are dishonest, ya know? Whether you are lying to people or stealing stuff, it's just not cool. One time one of my friends was ripping some music from a band I really like, and I said, "Whoa, bro, you're basically stealing from these artists. They put all this time and money and effort into making this album, and now you are just copying their music without paying them for it. It's like you're thievin' ten bucks out of their wallet." He asked me if I wanted a copy of the songs, and I told him no, that I would buy them if I wanted them. My buddy thought it was funny and was, like, "Hey, Dirk, relax a little, man, it's no big deal." But I think it is a big deal. Treating other people with some respect is important, and being dishonest isn't giving them the dignity they deserve.

Katie: Dirk, look at you go. I didn't expect that from you.

 Dirk: Yeah, I surprise people every now and then. Little more goin' on in this soul than people think sometimes.

Thanks, Dirk. What else did you guys learn about the telestial kingdom? What did you learn about what it is like?

 David: D&C 76:109 says that the number of people who go to the telestial will be as "innumerable as the stars" in heaven or "the sand upon the seashore." That's a lot of people.

That *is* a lot of people. But keep in mind how many children of God there are, have been, and have yet to be born. I don't want you to get the idea that most of God's children are murdering adulterers who will go to the telestial kingdom. But we'll clarify that a little later.

 Trevor: Verse 86 is pretty serious. It says that these guys will never get to enjoy the presence of God or Jesus, but only the Holy Ghost.

Lindsay: Verse 85 says that telestial people will have to wait until the last resurrection. When's the last resurrection?

The last resurrection will be at the end of the Millennium, or about 1,000 years after Christ comes again. The righteous will be resurrected when Jesus returns as part of the first resurrection, but the wicked—specifically the telestial people—will have to wait until the end of the Millennium to receive their resurrected bodies (see Revelation 20:5; LDS Bible Dictionary, "Resurrection," 761).

 Lindsay: That's a long old wait.

 Mikayla: I heard that Joseph Smith said that the telestial kingdom is so beautiful that you would kill yourself to go there.

I have heard that too. But there is no known reference I can find that supports Joseph Smith saying you would kill yourself to get to the telestial kingdom. That may just be Mormon folklore that has gone around. Although Joseph Smith never said that, he did say something that is mind-boggling about the glory of the telestial kingdom, and it is in section 76. Look at verse 89. Will you read that one, Mikayla?

Mikayla: "And thus we saw, in the heavenly vision, the glory of the telestial, which surpasses all understanding."

Can you imagine that? The glory of the telestial kingdom is beyond our ability to comprehend. How kind and merciful is our God! Even those who are sinful and rebellious, who will have to pay to justice the price of their rebellion by themselves, will receive from the Lord a kingdom of incomprehensible glory.

Katie: That doesn't seem quite fair. Why would he reward the most evil people with something good?

Another good question, Katie. Keep in mind that everyone who is ever born on this earth, at one point, chose to agree to God's plan.

Katie: You mean in the premortal life?

Exactly. The modern prophets teach us that "in the premortal realm, spirit sons and daughters knew and worshiped God as their Eternal Father and accepted His plan."[4] The book of Abraham tells us that all those who accepted God's plan and "who [kept] their first estate shall be added upon" with a kingdom of glory (Abraham 3:26). Also, flip over in your scriptures and let's look at verse 110 of section 76. It says that even the wicked who are sent to the telestial kingdom will eventually "bow the knee" and "confess" that Jesus is the Christ. Our Savior is so kind and good, He is so merciful that He rewards even the wicked with a kingdom of glory for accepting the plan in the beginning, and acknowledging His divinity in the end—even though they might have been rebellious in mortality. This doesn't mean that the telestial people will get away without any punishment for their disobedience to the laws of God. They will still pay the price and suffer for their sins in the spirit world as they await the resurrection. The difference is that we believe their time in hell will eventually come to an end and they will mercifully be assigned a kingdom of glory.

 Lindsay: Yeah, check this out. I looked this up in the Bible Dictionary under "Hell": "In latter-day revelation hell is spoken of in at least two senses. One is the temporary abode in the spirit world of those who were disobedient in this mortal life. . . . Hell, as thus defined, will have an end, when all the captive spirits have paid the price of their sins and enter into a degree of glory after their resurrection."[5]

Great reference, Lindsay, thanks. Listen to what Elder John A. Widtsoe said about what the wicked will receive in the telestial kingdom: "The book [Doctrine and Covenants] explains clearly that the lowest glory to which man is assigned is so glorious as to be beyond the understanding of man. It is a doctrine fundamental in Mormonism that the meanest [meaning the *lowest*] sinner, in the final judgment, will receive a glory which is beyond human understanding, which is so great that we are unable to describe it adequately."[6]

 Trevor: If the telestial kingdom is so great, it makes me wonder how sweet the terrestrial and celestial kingdoms will be.

You're right, Trevor. Take a look at D&C 76:91.

 Justin: It says: "And thus we saw the glory of the terrestrial which excels in all things the glory of the telestial, even in glory, and in power, and in might, and in dominion."

Olivia: What does it say about how great the celestial kingdom will be?

It seems there aren't even words for it. Look at D&C 76:92. All Joseph Smith can say after seeing the beauty and glory of the telestial and terrestrial kingdoms is that the celestial "excels in all things." I don't think we can comprehend the glory and beauty of the celestial kingdom. It is beyond anything earthly we have to compare or describe it with.

 Mikayla: I hope I can find out for myself one day how great the celestial kingdom will be. That is, if I make it. But at least I know the telestial kingdom is going to be pretty amazing too.

Mikayla, sorry to break it to you, but from what we just learned I don't think you're telestial material. Think about what we just studied and discussed: those who will inherit the lowest kingdom are those who *never* accept, and willfully reject, the gospel, in this life and the next; unrepentant adulterers; fornicators; whoremongers; murderers; and those who love lying and dishonesty. Does that describe you, Mikayla, or any of you good youth of the Church?

 David: That doesn't fit the profile of anyone I personally know, let alone my LDS friends.

So, after what we have discovered, do any of you in this class still think you are going to the telestial kingdom?

 Mikayla: Not anymore.

 Lindsay: Not really. Not when you look at it like that.

 Dirk: Bro, you are giving me hope! I've moved up from outer darkness and the telestial kingdom in just a few class periods!

Hopefully you 5 percent who thought you were going to the telestial feel a little better. But let's not be satisfied with simply avoiding the telestial kingdom. Almost half of you youth of Zion still think you are going to the terrestrial kingdom. Next class we'll study who really qualifies for that glory and see if we can clarify some misunderstanding there as well.

CLASS #5

The Terrestrial Kingdom

Of the three heavens, the terrestrial kingdom is usually the most common place where Latter-day Saint youth think they will spend eternity. If we review our stats from the beginning of the class, over 40 percent of you thought you would go to there. Now, help refresh my memory of why some of you assigned yourself to that kingdom.

 Dirk: It's like we've said before, man. We're just normal kids, ya know? Not bad, but not great. Not murderers, but not keeping every commandment all the time. I mean, dude, let's face it, we mess up sometimes.

 Katie: One reason that some say they are going to the terrestrial is because maybe they are being humble. They don't want to be boastful and prideful and say, "Yeah, I'll make it to the celestial kingdom." Like it's easy for them or they are the best or something. Maybe they just want to show a little humility.

I can appreciate that point, Katie, and maybe some people *are* just trying to be humble when they say they don't think they'll make it to the celestial kingdom. But I believe it is more than that. I sense that most don't really understand what is required of them to make it to the celestial kingdom. They set the bar too high—almost unrealistically high. Using our analogy from earlier, they think the celestial kingdom is an Ivy League school with impossible entrance requirements, but they don't really understand what the entrance requirements are.

And you who are in this class are no different from the hundreds of other active LDS youth across the country I have asked to respond to this same question. Remember, these are kids who are *actively engaged* in the gospel. They are youth similar to you and who are attending their church meetings, partaking of the sacrament, and are involved in Mutual and seminary. They accept and fulfill callings, do service projects, study their scriptures, pray consistently, and are trying to do what is right. They feel remorse and usually repent when they do something wrong. Is that the kind of person who will go the terrestrial kingdom? Well, let's see. Take a minute and study D&C 76:71–80, 91, 97, looking for the same things as before:

(a) the attributes of those who will go to the terrestrial kingdom, and

(b) what it will be like in that kingdom.

Let your answers start flying when you find them.

 Olivia: Is that all the verses, just those few?

Yep. Isn't that interesting that in a revelation that spans 119 verses, only 12 of them are dedicated to the terrestrial kingdom? In comparison, 16 are spent on sons of perdition, 18 verses on the telestial, and 26 verses on the celestial kingdom. It appears that we dwell more on the terrestrial kingdom than the Lord does. Perhaps we should be focusing more on the celestial kingdom since that is where the majority of the emphasis is placed. From the few verses on the terrestrial kingdom that we do have, what did you find?

 Lindsay: Verse 72 says terrestrial people are ones who "died without law." But I don't get what that means.

 Justin: It means they lived in some uncivilized place where there are no governments or laws or anything, like in a state of total anarchy. Sweet.

 David: Actually, isn't that verse referring to the law of the gospel of Christ? I think that verse is talking about those people who lived and died without the gospel, no matter where they lived.

Justin, thanks for your comment. What do you think about what David said?

Justin: David's the future prophet, so I guess what he said is probably right.

Well, he is right, and so are you. Not that anarchy is sweet, but this verse is referring to all those, in different countries and places and corners of the world, who lived without understanding the law of Christ—thus they "died without law."

Olivia: So I'm confused. Does that mean that if you didn't have the chance to become a member of the Church during your lifetime, that the highest kingdom you can go to is the terrestrial one? So when we do baptisms for the dead, they can't go to the celestial?

Katie: That can't be right. That doesn't sound very fair.

Lindsay: Well, girl, if it isn't fair, then it isn't right, because God is fair.

It might seem a little confusing, but remember what was revealed to Joseph Smith in D&C 137:7–8 about those who died without the opportunity to accept the gospel. Let's turn there and reread those verses so we are clear:

"Thus came the voice of the Lord unto me, saying: All who have died without a knowledge of this gospel, who would have received it if they had been permitted to tarry, shall be heirs of the celestial kingdom of God;

"Also all that shall die henceforth without a knowledge of it, who would have received it with all their hearts, shall be heirs of that kingdom."

It is evident from these verses that those who do not have the opportunity to receive the gospel in mortality but do so in the spirit world can inherit the celestial kingdom and aren't limited to the terrestrial kingdom. If you look at the next verses in section 76, verses 72–74, it clarifies more who the Lord is referring to concerning those who "died without law" and who will go to the terrestrial kingdom.

Mikayla: Yeah. Verse 74 says the terrestrial are those "who received not the testimony of Jesus in the flesh, but afterwards received it." So, it's like people who willfully reject living the gospel in this life, after having received it. Then, after this life when they go to the spirit world, they decide they want to be part of the gospel again.

Good insight, Mikayla. You sound just like Elder Bruce R. McConkie. He said: "Those who reject the gospel in this life and then receive it in the spirit world go not to the celestial, but to the terrestrial kingdom."[1] They key is that they had the gospel at one point in their life and knew it was true. Not only did they know it is true and had testimonies of it but they had a clear knowledge and understanding of its truthfulness, born of the Spirit. If someone has a deep, clear, spiritual knowledge and understanding of the gospel and then willfully turns from it in rebellion and decides not to follow it until the next life, he or she will apparently go to the terrestrial kingdom.

Trevor: Verse 79 says something that is kinda like that. It says that the terrestrial kingdom is for those "who are not valiant in the testimony of Jesus." So they had received Christ and His gospel at one point, but didn't stay with it and stick it out. They kind of gave up in the third or fourth quarter and quit the game.

Mikayla: Or first quarter if you are playing, Trevor.

Trevor: Because I'm so dominant the game is over by the first quarter, that's all.

 Katie: Careful, Trevor—isn't pride also one of the sins that leads people to the terrestrial kingdom?

Well, Katie isn't far from the truth. Our Savior gave a great parable in Matthew 13, called the parable of the sower, which describes why some people reject the "seed" or the word of God, and why others accept it. One of the four groups He describes in that parable are those who receive the word, or have testimonies, but then "the care of this world, and the deceitfulness of riches, choke the word, and he becometh unfruitful" (Matthew 13:22). In other words, the pride and cares and things of the world crowd out living the gospel, and such people fall away. So pride can lead to the terrestrial kingdom if the prideful cares of this world lead us away from accepting and being active in the gospel.

 Olivia: Verse 75 says something like that. It says terrestrial people are ones who are "blinded by the craftiness of men." I think that means they aren't wicked people, like telestial people. In fact, the same verse says that terrestrial people "are honorable men of the earth," so they aren't bad, but maybe just distracted from following Christ.

Good comment, Olivia. I think this verse could refer to members of the Church who get blinded by and love the things of the world most: money, fame, power, popularity, good looks, entertainment, and things like that. They are indeed good, decent, respectable, or in other words "honorable" people, but they are more concerned about pursuing or having worldly things than they are about living the Savior's gospel, and they know it. President Joseph Fielding Smith said, "Into the terrestrial will go all those who are honorable, who have been morally clean, *but who would not receive the gospel.*"[2] The words the prophet uses, *"would not,"* are significant, implying that terrestrial people have the opportunity to embrace the fulness of the everlasting gospel but refuse to receive it.

 Justin: So does that mean that everyone who doesn't invite the missionaries in and hear them will go to the terrestrial kingdom? Because I have this friend who lives next door, and he isn't a member of the Church. I spend a lot of time at his house because his mom is cool. Sometimes he asks me what Mormons believe and about things we do, so I tell him. One day I was over there and the missionaries came by. My friend's mom looked through the peep hole to see who it was, but didn't answer the door because she was really busy vacuuming their house getting ready for a party and didn't have time to talk to them. So does that mean she rejected her chance to hear the gospel and will go to the terrestrial kingdom?

Well, that seems to be too heavy an eternal price to pay for clean carpet. Just because a missionary knocks on the door of someone and they don't invite them in doesn't mean that was their one and only chance to hear the gospel and they are eternally doomed. I don't believe God works like that.

Maybe the person heard some false rumors about Mormons and because of their prejudices they were scared of the missionaries, so they didn't invite them in. Or maybe they were sick that day and didn't feel well enough to invite them in. There are many situations that prevent good people from hearing and receiving the gospel—things that I am confident the Lord, in His wisdom, will take into consideration.

 Justin: I had some Jehovah's Witness missionaries come to my house once and I didn't answer the door because I was in the middle of an intense video game that I didn't want to stop.

And, Justin, suppose that you weren't a member of the true

Church, and that those missionaries weren't Jehovah's Witnesses, but that they were LDS missionaries with the fulness of the gospel to offer to you, and instead you played video games. Do you think it would be fair for a loving God to say, "Well, there go the missionaries. Justin blew it because he was too focused on passing level four on his gaming system. Too bad for him"?

 Justin: No, that wouldn't seem quite fair.

Remember, the Lord will give everyone the chance, whether in this life or the next, to be taught so completely that the Spirit will be able to witness to them the truthfulness of the gospel of Jesus Christ so they can receive it.[3] It is only after having the Spirit witness and provide spiritual knowledge and understanding that something is true—and then refusing to follow it—that we damn ourselves.

 Dirk: Whoa, teacher just swore.

 Katie: No, he didn't, Dirk. "Damn" means to stop something. You know, like a water dam? It stops the water from going forward. When the scriptures say someone is "damned," it just means they can't progress anymore.

 Dirk: Thanks, Kate. Now I know how to swear properly.

I appreciate the clarification, Katie. I wouldn't want Dirk to lose his testimony because he thought his teacher had a scriptural swearing problem. Katie is right. Terrestrial people technically will be damned because they can't go on to the highest kingdom, the celestial, so their progression is stopped.

 Trevor: Hey, about that. I heard that we can progress from kingdom to kingdom in the next life, though. So, even if I was to go to the terrestrial kingdom, eventually I could be

un-damned and progress and move into the celestial kingdom. Isn't that right?

Lindsay: Yeah, I have heard the same thing.

Katie: So have I.

Dirk: The only thing I keep hearing is people swearing in this
class.

David: I've heard that idea too, but I don't think you can progress upward from kingdom to kingdom. In Abraham 3 it says
that God sent us here to earth to prove us. He didn't say He
would prove us in the eternal kingdoms. We earn our eternal
reward while on this earth.

David, you are spot on. The verses you are referencing are
Abraham 3:24–26. The Lord says in verse 26 that "they who keep their
second estate shall have glory added upon their heads for ever and
ever." Our first estate was when we lived and our faith was tried in the
premortal existence. Our second estate is our testing during our life
here on earth and in the spirit world. The scriptures don't say anything
about a third estate, or our resurrected state, as a time of testing and
proving.

Lindsay: Isn't there a Book of Mormon scripture mastery verse
that teaches the same principle? I think it is in Alma 34. Yeah,
here it is: Alma 34:32.

See, right there is one of the reasons we have those scripture mastery verses. They come in handy. Read it to us, Lindsay.

Lindsay: It says, "For behold, this life is the time for men to
prepare to meet God; yea, behold the day of this life is the day
for men to perform their labors."

So what truth do you think that verse is teaching?

 Lindsay: I think it is pretty clear. It says "this life" is our time to prepare to meet God, not the next life after the resurrection.

President Spencer W. Kimball said it plainly: "After a person has been assigned to his place in the kingdom, either in the telestial, the terrestrial, or the celestial, or to his exaltation, he will never advance from his assigned glory to another glory. That is eternal!"[4] From what we know, the concept of "eternal progression" is limited to those who make it to the highest level of the celestial kingdom and have an eternal marriage (see D&C 132:19). Speaking of those who are not sealed in the temple and who haven't received the highest degree of the celestial kingdom, the Lord says in D&C 131:4 that they "cannot have an increase." Part of eternal progression has to do with having an eternal marriage, which those in the terrestrial and telestial kingdoms won't have.

 Trevor: You mean if I don't make it the highest part of the celestial kingdom, I won't be married and I'll end up being single forever?

 Mikayla: Can you say "eternal singles ward," Trevor?

Well, if Trevor decides to reject temple marriage, that is exactly what he'll be saying.

With that, let's recap who will go to the terrestrial kingdom then. The book *Gospel Principles* has a good summary. Let's read from there. Katie, will you read?

 Katie: "[Terrestrial people] are they who rejected the gospel on earth but afterward received it in the spirit world. These are the honorable people on the earth who were blinded to the gospel of Jesus Christ by the craftiness of men. These are also they who received the gospel and a testimony of Jesus but then were not valiant. They will be visited by Jesus Christ but not by our Heavenly Father. . . . They will not be part of eternal families; they will live separately and singly forever."[5]

So does that sound like a fitting description for 40 percent of you sitting in this class?

David: Not really. I mean, if we were rejecting the gospel and being blinded by the world and stuff, we wouldn't be going to church and reading our scriptures and praying. We wouldn't be enrolled in seminary and going to Young Men and Young Women activities. We wouldn't be repenting and striving to do what is right. If we weren't valiant in our testimony of Christ, I doubt we would be active in the gospel and doing any of those things at all. It seems to me that the terrestrial kingdom is more for those members of the Church who have willfully rejected the gospel after having received it—or who love the world more than Christ. It doesn't seem to be for people like us who are trying our best to receive the gospel, even if we mess up every now and then.

So can we actually entertain the thought that, even though we aren't perfect, you and I can still go to the celestial kingdom? Next class we'll study what section 76 says about imperfect members of the Church like us—who love the Lord and are trying to do what is right, and what kingdom they will receive.

Dirk: Give me hope, brother.

CLASS #6

The Celestial Kingdom

If I drew two triangles divided in thirds, with the celestial kingdom being the top of the triangle and the telestial kingdom being the bottom of the triangle, which one do you think best represents how many people will be in each kingdom?

 Olivia: I think most people would say the first one.

I think most people would say the first one as well. Why do you think some people automatically assume that there will be many, many more of God's children in the telestial or terrestrial kingdoms than in the celestial kingdom?

 Olivia: I said the first triangle because it seems harder to get into the celestial kingdom, like more effort, than the other two.

 Katie: I agree with Olivia because there aren't that many members of the Church in the world. I mean, yeah, there are like 13 million Mormons or something like that, but there are

46

over 7 billion people on this planet. If you do the math, that means that 99.9 percent of the world's population *isn't* LDS.

You are right, Katie: when you do the math there aren't that many members of God's Church on the earth. At least not right now, anyway. However, how many of the 7 billion currently on earth have really had the Spirit witness to them that the restored gospel is true and have had the opportunity to be baptized and receive it?

David: Probably not many of them. We still don't even have missionaries in China, which is one-third of the world's population.

I'm not sure if we can do the math regarding how many of God's children will be in the celestial kingdom based on what percent of the living population is LDS.

Katie: Why not?

Well, for a lot of reasons: Think of how many of God's children who never heard the gospel, past and present, will accept the gospel in the spirit world and be worthy of the celestial kingdom (see D&C 137:7–8). Think of how many will accept the gospel on earth as the Church continues to grow and fill the world. Think how many will join the Church when Dirk, Justin, Trevor, David, and other similar young men are serving their missions. Or, for that matter, how many will join the Church as a result of some of you young women going on missions. Think of how many will accept the gospel during the Millennium, when error and confusion will be removed and "the earth shall be full of the knowledge of the Lord" (Isaiah 11:9). Think of how many billions of children will be born in the thousand years of the Millennium who will live and die without ever committing a sin due to Satan being bound (see D&C 45:55, 58).[1] Add to these all the millions of children in the earth's history who have died before the age of eight, who are automatic heirs of the celestial kingdom (see D&C 137:10). Think of all the

47

mentally disabled who are not susceptible to temptation. Add in all the righteous who have loved the Lord and followed His ways in the Bible and the Book of Mormon. Entire cities, such as Enoch's, have been translated!

 Dirk: Dude, that's a lot of dudes that might go to heaven. And dudettes. Sorry, ladies.

Do we really think that God's eternal plan, His perfect plan, is a plan designed to exalt and save only a small handful in the celestial kingdom? God's plan is not a plan of failure; it is a plan of successful salvation! Elder Quentin L. Cook said that it is an "incorrect doctrine that most of mankind [will] be doomed to eternal hell."[2] In fact, Elder Bruce R. McConkie once said to teachers of youth: "'You tell your students that far more of our Father's children will be exalted than we think!'"[3]

 Trevor: Really?

Yes, really. In the New Testament, the Apostle John had a revelation where he saw exalted people from all nations. All of us who see the heavenly triangle as "bottom-heavy" might be surprised to know how many people John saw in the celestial kingdom. Olivia, will you read Revelation 7:9 for us?

 Olivia: Sure. It says, "I beheld, and, lo, a great multitude, which no man could number, of all nations, and kindreds, and people, and tongues, stood before the throne, and before the Lamb, clothed with white robes."

So how many were in the celestial kingdom?

 Olivia: There were so many that John couldn't even count them.

So should the triangle be bottom-heavy or top-heavy?

 Trevor: Maybe it should be top-heavy. Maybe we do make it harder in our heads to get into heaven than Christ really says it is.

Well, let's see. How about we take a look at what the Lord outlines as the actual requirements to make it to heaven by reading D&C 76:50–53? As you read these verses on the celestial kingdom, once again highlight each of the specific requirements you find.

"And again we bear record—for we saw and heard, and this is the testimony of the gospel of Christ concerning them who shall come forth in the resurrection of the just—

"They are they who received the testimony of Jesus, and believed on his name and were baptized after the manner of his burial, being buried in the water in his name, and this according to the commandment which he has given—

"That by keeping the commandments they might be washed and cleansed from all their sins, and receive the Holy Spirit by the laying on of the hands of him who is ordained and sealed unto this power;

"And who overcome by faith, and are sealed by the Holy Spirit of promise, which the Father sheds forth upon all those who are just and true."

So what did you find? What requirements for celestial glory do you see?

 David: It looks like the first one is in verse 51, where it says we need to receive the testimony of Jesus.

Good, David. What do you think that phrase means exactly?

 David: I assume that means that you have a testimony of Christ, that he is the Son of God and the Savior of the world.

Mikayla: Well, isn't that kind of what the second requirement is, in verse 51, that we believe on His name?

They are similar, yes, but still different. What do you think is the difference between having a *testimony* of something, and *believing* on it? Notice the word is to believe *on* it and not *in* it?

 Trevor: I think I see what the difference is. It's like the difference between knowing something and doing something about it. I might know that it's good for me to lift weights, exercise, and eat right, but that doesn't mean that I necessarily do it. Actually, *I* do, but some people don't. Same with this. I think the second requirement to believe "on" His name means we do something about our testimony of Jesus.

Trevor, you said if we believe *on* Jesus' name that we will do something. What are some of the things we will do?

 Trevor: I don't know. Like, we will just do what He says.

 Lindsay: Well, if you look at the third requirement for the celestial kingdom in verse 51, it says that we will be baptized. We will get baptized and take His name on us if we believe on His name. I kinda think the first requirement, to have a testimony of Jesus, is like the first principle of the gospel: you know—faith. The second requirement, to believe on His name, could be repentance, because the third requirement is obviously baptism by immersion. It is like it goes in the same order as our Articles of Faith.

That's a great insight, Lindsay. So, looking at verse 52, what is the next requirement after faith, repentance, and baptism? It says that by keeping the commandments (faith) and repenting of our sins (the first and second principles of the gospel), we are washed (baptism) and then cleansed from all our sins by this last requirement . . .

 Olivia: Receiving the Holy Ghost.

Exactly. Anything else?

 Trevor: Well, verse 52 also says that we need to keep the commandments in order to qualify for baptism and the gift of the Holy Ghost.

Good, Trevor. Thanks for reemphasizing the point that being willing to keep the commandments, exercising faith, and repenting are what qualify us for ordinances such as baptism and the reception of the Holy Ghost, which is what verse 52 teaches.

 David: Aren't there some other requirements in verse 53—that we "overcome by faith" and are "sealed by the Holy Spirit of promise"?

Yes, there are. Good eye. What do you interpret "overcoming by faith" to be, after we are baptized and have received the Holy Ghost?

 Dirk: I see it as like sticking it out, you know? Like staying with it and not giving up. What is the word they always use in the scriptures that sounds so painful . . . ?

 Katie: Endure.

 Dirk: Yeah, "endure to the end" is the phrase I always hear in Church. I think that is what "overcoming by faith" could mean after we are baptized and receive the Holy Ghost. It's like one time when I was on the mountain and hit a big kicker and lifted off the tranny to pull a backside 720 grab, but didn't stick with it and see it through. I just gave up at the 450 mark and froze halfway and was toast and hit the lip. Talk about painful. Same with the gospel: you gotta stay with it once you commit.

 Katie: All of a sudden I feel like I'm in a foreign language class.

I get it, Dirk. Not the snowboard lingo, but the analogy. What you guys are saying sounds like Nephi telling us to commit by repenting, being baptized, receiving the Holy Ghost, and then seeing it through by enduring to the end (see 2 Nephi 31:12–20). Actually, what you guys just outlined from section 76—faith in the Lord Jesus Christ, repentance, baptism by immersion, and receiving the Holy Ghost—isn't just an article of faith about the gospel; it is the *definition* of "the gospel." Find and highlight how our Savior Himself described "the gospel" when He taught the Nephites in 3 Nephi 27:20–21. Justin, will you read that for the class?

 Justin: "Now this is the commandment: Repent, all ye ends of the earth, and come unto me and be baptized in my name, that ye may be sanctified by the reception of the Holy Ghost, that ye may stand spotless before me at the last day. Verily, verily, I say unto you, this is my gospel."

In an earlier verse in this same chapter, verse 16, the Lord added "endureth to the end" after baptism and the Holy Ghost as the last requirement. "This is my gospel," our Savior said: Faith, repentance, baptism, Holy Ghost, endure to the end. Katie, can you read what our Lord said to those who "live" these five fundamental aspects of the gospel in 3 Nephi 27:22?

 Katie: "Therefore, if ye do these things blessed are ye, for ye shall be lifted up at the last day."

In other words, you'll make it to the celestial kingdom.

Trevor: That's it? That's all we need to do?

Yep, that's it. Sometimes we make it a little more complicated than it really is.

Lindsay: But we didn't really address what it means to be "sealed by the Holy Spirit of promise" as part of the requirements in section 76, verse 53. What does that phrase mean?

That is a great question. The Holy Spirit of promise has been described by prophets as the Lord's "stamp of approval" for covenant-making Latter-day Saints.[4] In other words, after we have exercised faith in Jesus Christ, repented in His name, and have been baptized and confirmed into His church, the Holy Spirit of promise is what ratifies, or authorizes, all the ordinances we have done in the name of Christ. It basically is the final "all clear" stamp that ensures all of the promised blessings of the covenants we are making will be received.[5]

Lindsay: That makes sense. So it is kind of like the Holy Ghost agreeing that we have kept our part of the covenant.

That is right. So, you guys, this is the moment of truth. Let's recap what the Lord just told us in section 76 about what it takes to qualify for the celestial kingdom. As we review these requirements, ask yourselves, "Have I met those qualifications?"

1. Receive the testimony of Jesus (have faith in Him).
2. Believe *on* His name (repent and be willing to keep the commandments).
3. Be baptized by authority (baptism by immersion).
4. Receive the Holy Spirit (laying on of hands for the gift of the Holy Ghost).

5. Overcome by faith (endure to the end; or in other words, remain "valiant" in your testimony).

How many of you meet those requirements right now?

David: So far I have.

Katie: I think I do.

Lindsay: Man, when you put it that way it seems so simple.

Dirk: Dude, even I have done those things!

Mikayla: Wait a minute. I thought that we had to be married in the temple in order to go to the celestial kingdom. Don't we? That is why I voted earlier that I didn't think I would make it to the celestial kingdom—because if I died today, I don't have a temple marriage yet, so I wouldn't make it.

That is a common point of confusion I have heard from other youth. Let's clarify that right now by looking at this diagram as we read D&C 131:1–4. It says:

"In the celestial glory there are three heavens or degrees;

"And in order to obtain the highest, a man must enter into this order of the priesthood [meaning the new and everlasting covenant of marriage];

"And if he does not, he cannot obtain it.

"He may enter into the other, but that is the end of his kingdom; he cannot have an increase."

So what truths do you see taught there about your question, Mikayla?

Mikayla: Well, it looks like in the celestial kingdom there are three divisions and to get into the highest one, you need to be sealed in the temple. So, like, you don't need to have a temple marriage to make it into the other parts of the celestial kingdom? That doesn't seem right because the Church puts so much emphasis on temple marriage.

To put it bluntly, no, we don't need to be sealed in the temple to qualify for the celestial kingdom *as a whole*. Not from what the Prophet Joseph just taught us in section 131, anyway. Now before we misunderstand this all-important point, let me state clearly that being married in the temple is *the single most important thing* we can ever do on this earth. Of all the millions of decisions a Latter-day Saint makes throughout a lifetime, the most important is to marry the right person, in the right place, by the right authority.[6] Everything the Church does, all of its programs, is geared toward pointing us to the temple and having a faithful temple marriage.[7] President Spencer W. Kimball said:

"Any of you would go around the world for the sealing ordinance if you knew its importance, if you realized how great it is. No distance, no shortage of funds, no situation would ever keep you from being married in the holy temple of the Lord."[8]

 Katie: If it's so important, then why isn't it listed in section 76 as a requirement to be saved in the celestial kingdom?

Because that's just it, Katie: you don't need temple marriage to be *saved* in the celestial kingdom, but you do need it to be *exalted*.

 Olivia: I don't get it. What's the difference between being saved and being exalted?

 David: I think I can explain that. Being "saved" means that we can go to the celestial kingdom. We are saved from our sins and death and can live in God's presence. But it doesn't mean that we become like God, which is what it means to be exalted.

Right on, David. Does that make sense, Olivia? The purpose of life, and the entire plan of salvation, can be summed up in four words: *to become like God.*[9] That is ultimately why we are here on earth. We are here to gain the divine attributes that God has. One essential thing God has is an eternal marriage.[10] As "The Family: A Proclamation to the World" states, we are the children of "heavenly parents,"[11] children of a Heavenly *Father and Mother.* That is why Joseph Smith said that if we are to enter into the highest division of the celestial kingdom, or, in other words, if we are to become like God and be *exalted,* we need to be sealed in the temple. Elder Russell M. Nelson of the Quorum of the Twelve has taught:

"To be exalted—or to gain exaltation—refers to the highest state of happiness and glory in the celestial realm. . . .

"No man in this Church can obtain the highest degree of celestial glory without a worthy woman who is sealed to him. This temple ordinance enables eventual exaltation for both of them."[12]

To become like God, or to be *exalted,* we need to be sealed in the temple. Exaltation is what our Heavenly Father wants for us (see Moses 1:39), and it should be our goal. However, in order to be *saved* in the celestial kingdom of God and enjoy God's presence, we simply need to do what section 76 teaches: have faith, repent, get baptized, receive the gift of the Holy Ghost, and endure to the end. Baptism is the door to *salvation* in the celestial kingdom (see John 3:5), and temple marriage is the door to *exaltation* in the celestial kingdom (see D&C 131:1–4).

 Katie: So if I get married outside the temple, I can still be with my husband in the celestial kingdom, just not in the highest part?

I didn't say that and neither do the scriptures. Turn to section 132 with me. Let's read D&C 132:15–17 to answer Katie's question.

"Therefore, if a man marry him a wife in the world, and he marry her not by me nor by my word, and he covenant with her so long as he is in the world and she with him, their covenant and marriage are not of force when they are dead, and when they are out of the world; therefore, they are not bound by any law when they are out of the world.

"Therefore, when they are out of the world they neither marry nor are given in marriage; but are appointed angels in heaven, which angels are ministering servants, to minister for those who are worthy of a far more, and an exceeding, and an eternal weight of glory.

"For these angels did not abide my law; therefore, they cannot be enlarged, but remain separately and singly, without exaltation, in their saved condition, to all eternity; and from henceforth are not gods, but are angels of God forever and ever."

Katie, what truths do you see that are taught in that verse that might answer your question?

Katie: Well, it looks like those who don't marry in the temple can still be in the celestial kingdom, but they won't be married. They will be angels in the celestial kingdom, and will be single for eternity.

Exactly. Notice the words *saved* and *exaltation* in the revelation that we have been discussing: "[They] remain separately and singly, without *exaltation,* in their *saved* condition, to all eternity" (emphasis added). According to section 132, then, those who are exalted in the celestial kingdom will "be gods" (vs. 20), and those who are saved in the celestial kingdom "are appointed angels" (vs. 16) to God and others who are exalted.

Lindsay: So, does that mean if I die when I am young or before I have the chance to be married in the temple, that I will have to be an angel forever in the celestial kingdom? Because I don't want to have to be servin' Trevor for all eternity simply because he had the chance to be married in the temple and I didn't!

Maybe a quote from Elder Dallin H. Oaks will help. He said, "The Lord has promised that in the eternities no blessing will be denied his sons and daughters who keep the commandments . . . and desire what is right."[13] As we mentioned earlier in our discussion, Joseph Smith taught: "All who have died without a knowledge of this gospel, who would have received it if they had been permitted to tarry, shall be heirs of the celestial kingdom of God" (D&C 137:7). In regards to your question, Lindsay, we could take the principle taught in that verse and say that all who have died without the opportunity to be married in the temple, who would have received it, will have that opportunity one day. You don't need to worry about being an angel forever if you die before you get the chance to be married in the temple.

 Lindsay: Good thing, because that wouldn't be fair.

You're right, and I testify that God is fair and will give all His children an opportunity for exaltation. With that, let's recap the requirements for the celestial kingdom that we have discussed:
1. Receive the testimony of Jesus—faith.
2. Believe *on* His name—repent and keep the commandments.
3. Be baptized by authority—baptism by immersion.
4. Receive the Holy Spirit—laying on of hands for the gift of the Holy Ghost.
5. Overcome by faith—endure to the end or be "valiant" in our testimonies.

When we look at that list of our requirements from section 76, I notice that one giant word is missing from what we thought was required from us: *perfection.* Nowhere in those celestial expectations does the Lord mention that *we* need to be perfect in order to qualify for the celestial kingdom.

 Katie: Yeah, we didn't read anywhere that we need to be perfect, did we?

That is the key, Katie. *We* don't need to be perfect, but someone else does. We'll find out who that someone is next class.

CLASS #7

The Perfect Atonement

As we discussed earlier, one of the main reasons that some of us don't think we are going to heaven is that as members of the Church we think that *we* need to be the ones who are perfect, that *we* need to be the ones who are sinless and spotless in order to go to the celestial kingdom. We reason: If the celestial kingdom is pure and holy—which it is—then *I* must be the one who has no sins and who remains holy by living a perfect life. And since none of us do live a perfect life, it becomes easy to say, "Well, I guess I am not celestial material because I have sins. I guess I won't make it." Then we assign ourselves to the terrestrial kingdom because that is where all the faithful-yet-imperfect Saints will go. Right?

 Olivia: I still don't understand, though, because what you just said is how I think sometimes. If heaven is spotless and perfect, but I'm not, then how can I be worthy to go there?

The key to this kind of perfection, for all of us, is found in D&C 76:69. In this verse, our Lord is talking about those who will inherit the celestial kingdom. Let's read this critically important verse and see what truths are taught there. "These are they who are just men made perfect through Jesus the mediator of the new covenant, who wrought out this perfect atonement through the shedding of his own blood."

 David: I see. We are not the ones who need to be perfect, meaning sinless, at all. Jesus is the only one who needed to be perfect and who was perfect. We are made perfect by His Atonement, like verse 69 says.

That is exactly right, David, and to be honest, that is probably one of the greatest truths we can come to believe in the entire gospel: WE don't need to be perfect to go to heaven because Jesus was perfect for us.

 Justin: But how does that work? How does Jesus' perfection make me perfect and worthy to go to the celestial kingdom?

First of all, let's discuss Jesus' perfect Atonement before we can understand how the Atonement makes us fit for the celestial kingdom. To understand Jesus' perfect Atonement in the Garden of Gethsemane, we need to go back to the first garden, the Garden of Eden.

 Mikayla: Like Adam and Eve you mean, that garden? Why would we need to go there to understand Jesus' Atonement?

I'll show you through a simple little experiment. I want to see who in the class can hold their breath for at least a minute. Ready, go!
Keep holdin' . . .
Keep holdin' it . . .
Almost there . . .
Okay, breathe.
Looks like most of you were able to do that one.

 Dirk: Hate to break it to ya, bro, but I gave out at around forty-five seconds.

That's all right, Dirk. The point wasn't whether or not you could do it for a minute; the real point was what you were thinking about while you couldn't breathe. So what were you thinking about?

Trevor: I was thinking about my eternal singles ward I don't want to be stuck in.

 Lindsay: All I was thinking about was when I could breathe again.

How many of you were thinking about breathing, along the lines of "All right, fifteen more seconds, then I can breathe again"?

 Katie: I was.

Interesting. And how many times, Katie, had you thought about breathing today, before we did our little exercise?

 Katie: None, really.

I would assume most of the rest of you were the same. You hadn't consciously thought at all about breathing until you couldn't breathe. You don't realize how much you need air until it is taken away from you.

 Katie: But what does not being able to breathe have to do with Jesus' Atonement?

Let me read you this quote from President Ezra Taft Benson, then you might understand a little more where I am going with this:

"Just as a man does not really desire food [or air] until he is hungry [or can't breathe], so he does not desire the salvation of Christ until he knows why he needs Christ.

"No one adequately and properly knows why he needs Christ until he understands and accepts the doctrine of the Fall and its effect upon all mankind."[1]

Understanding the Fall of Adam and Eve enables us to understand the need for a Redeemer and the Atonement and how that Atonement can make us perfect. When Adam and Eve partook of the forbidden fruit, they brought some major changes into the world. What were some of them?

Mikayla: They brought birth into the world. I know that the scriptures say that they couldn't have any kids while they were in the garden.

Okay, good. The verses you are referring to are in 2 Nephi 2:22–23, where it says that nothing would have ever changed or progressed, like the birth of a new child, had Adam and Eve not fallen. What else was brought about by the Fall?

Trevor: If they hadn't sinned, Adam and Eve would have never died. They would have lived forever. Like 2 Nephi 2:22 says, the Fall didn't just bring birth into the world, it also brought death.

Justin: And weren't they kicked out of the Garden of Eden as well because of what they did?

Yes, they were. Verse 19 in 2 Nephi 2 says: "And after Adam and Eve had partaken of the forbidden fruit they were driven out of the garden of Eden." Because of their transgression they were no longer able to live in the presence of the Lord.

Justin: I knew that answer because I know all about getting kicked out of the house because of transgressions.

We all know a little about being in the doghouse with our parents, Justin. The key is how you get back in, or how you regain your parents' approval. It isn't much different with our heavenly home.

Justin: It isn't? What do you mean?

Well, when Adam and Eve fell, they brought two things into the world that separate us from God's presence, or in other words, from being worthy to be in the celestial kingdom. Those two things are *sin* and *death*.[2] As God has no sin, and is an immortal being, the results of the Fall keep us from ever becoming like God or living with God. That is, unless sin and death are overcome. Do you see why we need to understand the Fall in order to understand the Atonement?

 Lindsay: I get it. The Atonement of Jesus Christ fixes the problems caused by the Fall: sin and death.

Exactly. So how and when did the Savior overcome the effects of sin?

 Lindsay: In the Garden of Gethsemane, when He paid the price for all our sins.

And what about death? When did He overcome death?

 Lindsay: On the cross, when He died and then was resurrected.

Turn to Mormon 9:12 to see how Mormon summarized it. "By Adam came the fall of man. And because of the fall of man came Jesus Christ, . . . and because of Jesus Christ came the redemption of man."

You see, because you and I are mortal, we will die. Because we are subject to the natural man, we all have sins and therefore, as Paul put it, "come short of the glory of God" (Romans 3:23). But Christ's Atonement fixes all that. Through Jesus' Resurrection, as we studied before, we will *all* be resurrected and become immortal. And through His suffering in the Garden of Gethsemane, He paid the price for our sins, so that we can be made blameless and clean before God and be fit for the celestial kingdom.

Trevor: What do you mean He "paid the price" of our sins. Do our sins have a cost, like money?

Our sins definitely do have a cost, but the cost isn't money. But since you brought it up, maybe money can help us understand the Atonement a little better. Trevor, have you ever been pulled over for speeding and received a speeding ticket?

 Trevor: Yeah, a few times. That's what I get for having a V-8 engine.

And what was the penalty of your "sin" of speeding?

 Trevor: Speeding isn't a sin, is it? If it is, I'm really not going to heaven.

Well, you are breaking a law of the land, aren't you? Speeding at minimum violates the laws of the land. And when the laws of the land are violated, there usually is a penalty attached to it.

 Trevor: I don't know, I think my ticket was like seventy-five bucks or something.

Suppose that every time we violated any sort of a law, speeding, illegally copying music, skipping a class at school, that we were given a fine, no matter if we were caught or not. Say that somehow each time a violation of the law occurred, a fine was automatically imposed, and the total sum just kept adding and adding up throughout your life.

 Mikayla: That would be the worst.

Dirk: I say bankruptcy for me, man. I couldn't pay it.

Well, eternal laws aren't much different. For every eternal law that is broken, what we term a "sin," there is a consequence or punishment attached to it. "Do the crime, do the time," so to speak. Lehi said in 2 Nephi 2:10 that the laws of God have a "punishment which is affixed" to them.

 Trevor: So what is the punishment?

Turn with me to D&C 19:15–17 to see what the punishment is:
"Therefore I command you to repent—repent, lest I smite you by the rod of my mouth, and by my wrath, and by my anger, and your sufferings be sore—how sore you know not, how exquisite you know not, yea, how hard to bear you know not.

"For behold, I, God, have suffered these things for all, that they might not suffer if they would repent;

"But if they would not repent they must suffer even as I."

 Trevor: It looks like the punishment for sin is suffering.

And from what those verses teach, it sounds like it is a kind of suffering we can't imagine. I don't know how it works, but apparently eternal justice demands that where there is sin committed, a penalty of intense suffering must be made to justice to pay or "atone" for that sin.

 Katie: That is, unless we repent. Because in verse 16 that we just read it says that Christ suffered for us, so we won't have to if we choose to repent.

Katie, you sound a little like Lehi. He put it this way in 2 Nephi 2:7: "Behold, [Christ] offereth himself a sacrifice for sin, to answer the ends of the law." Lehi's son Jacob taught that Christ's suffering and Atonement "satisfieth the demands of . . . justice" (2 Nephi 9:26).

 Mikayla: Well, why did Jesus have to suffer for us? He didn't do anything wrong. Why can't we just pay for our own sins and still go to heaven?

Those are great questions and deep ones as well. First of all, do you *want* to suffer for your own sins?

 Mikayla: No, of course not. But I still don't feel like it is fair that Jesus had to do it for me.

Remember, Jesus didn't *have* to do anything. He voluntarily chose to do it for us because He loves us. He knew that He was the only one who could do this. He was the only one who had such spiritual capacity to withstand every temptation and not sin (see D&C 20:22). Therefore, He was the only one who owed no debt to justice. Using money as an analogy, Jesus was the only one with a positive spiritual bank account, so He is the only one who can actually pay for all of us who are in debt because of our sins.

 Trevor: So it's like my speeding ticket. The cop told me if I couldn't pay the money then I had to go to traffic school and "suffer" there for a few hours. I didn't have a job because of football, so I didn't have any money. Luckily, my dad helped me pay for it. Now I owe him a summer full of lawnmowing.

That is a great parallel to us and Christ, Trevor. You and I are in debt to justice, and we have insufficient spiritual money to pay. Christ *can* pay, and He lovingly offers to pay the price of our sins for us. But we owe Him more than a summer of lawnmowing; we owe Him *everything* for that.

Another reason that Jesus *chose* to atone for us was that He was the only one with the ability to die and be resurrected. I don't care how hard you and I try; we can't resurrect ourselves, bringing ourselves back to life in immortal glory. Jesus had the power to resurrect

Himself, and He has the power to resurrect each of us, which He has promised to do.

 Justin: Why can Jesus bring Himself back to life but we can't?

Well, we don't know everything there is to know about that, but consider this: From His mortal mother, Mary, Jesus inherited the ability to die. From His immortal Father, Jesus inherited the ability to live forever.[3] His perfect, sinless, and divinely inherited abilities made Him the only one who could complete a perfect Atonement, overcoming the debt of sin for us all, and conquering death for every living soul.

 David: Didn't Jesus also suffer not just the price for our sins, but also our sicknesses, suffering, emotional problems, and everything else, during the Atonement?

Yes, He did, David. Let's turn to Alma 7:11–13 and read some of the most enlightening verses ever written about Christ's sufferings. And while we're at it, notice how clearly these doctrines are taught in the Book of Mormon. As David reads these holy verses, highlight everything you can find that Jesus suffered in the Atonement.

 David: It says:
"And he shall go forth, suffering *pains* and *afflictions* and *temptations* of every kind; and this that the word might be fulfilled which saith he will take upon him the pains and the sicknesses of his people.

"And he will take upon him *death*, that he may loose the bands of death which bind his people; and he will take upon him their *infirmities,* that his bowels may be filled with mercy, according to the flesh, that he may know according to the flesh how to succor his people according to their infirmities.

"Now the Spirit knoweth all things; nevertheless the Son of God suffereth according to the flesh that he might take upon him the *sins* of his people, that he might blot out their transgressions according to the power of his deliverance; and now behold, this is the testimony which is in me" (emphasis added).

Pains, afflictions, temptations, sicknesses, death, infirmities, *and* sins. All of those things are what Jesus suffered in the Atonement. And why did He choose to do that? After all, being sick doesn't expel us from the celestial kingdom, neither does suffering physical and emotional pain. So why did our Savior choose to suffer those things as well?

Mikayla: Because He loves us and wants to understand us and know how to help us? I know He understands and loves me, anyway.

Trevor: Alma 7:12 that we just read says that Jesus suffered all of that so "that he may know according to the flesh how to succor his people." I think that means He did all of that so He can say, "I understand what you are going through. I have been there before." You know, so that He can relate and help us overcome our problems because He has felt them and overcome them.

Amen, brother. This is how Elder Merrill J. Bateman described it: "In the garden and on the cross, Jesus saw each of us and not only bore our sins but also experienced our deepest feelings so he would know how to comfort and strengthen us. . . .

"The Savior's atonement in the garden and on the cross is intimate as well as infinite—infinite in that it spans the eternities, intimate in that the Savior felt *each person's* pains, sufferings, and sicknesses. Consequently he knows how to carry our sorrows and relieve our burdens that we might be healed from within, be made whole persons, and receive everlasting joy in his kingdom."[4]

None of us can rightly say, "Nobody understands me," because there is One who does and probably understands you and me better than we understand ourselves. Jesus is so loving, and His Atonement is so perfect, that He not only overcame death and suffered the penalty of each of our sins, but overcame *everything* that is connected to the Fall of Adam: all our bad days, all our frustrations, all our temptations, all our sicknesses, our tears, our faults, and our failures. Elder Jeffrey R. Holland taught: "It was required, indeed it was central to the significance of the Atonement, that this perfect Son . . . had to know how the rest of humankind—us, all of us—would feel."[5] Have any of you ever felt or experienced this "understanding" power of the Atonement?

 Olivia: I have.

Would you mind sharing with the class what happened and how you felt understood because of the Atonement?

 Olivia: Sure. About two years ago, my parents got divorced. I remember feeling so scared because I didn't know what was going to happen. I didn't know who I would live with, or where I was going to go to school, and how it was going to all work out. I called my best friend to talk to her about it, and she was nice and listened and tried to offer advice, but I could tell she didn't really understand. I don't really blame her, though, because she came from a home where her mom and dad loved each other and had a happy marriage. She just couldn't relate to what I was going through. Anyway, one night I was having a really hard time and had been crying over my parents' divorce, and felt like I should pray, so I did. While I was praying, I got this overwhelming feeling that God was aware of me and my situation and that He loved me. More than anything I felt that I wasn't alone in what I was going through and that God understood me and would help me, which He has. That experience helped me know that God doesn't just love me; He understands me, and knowing that has helped me a lot.

Olivia, thanks so much for sharing that experience. That is exactly what I am talking about when I ask who has felt the understanding power of the Atonement. Jesus' perfect Atonement is an *understanding* Atonement because He gained perfect empathy for all of us through everything He felt and overcame in the garden, even things such as how it feels to have your parents get divorced.

 Katie: So Jesus has felt everything that I feel?

Everything.

 Katie: And He not only felt everything that I feel but suffered for every one of my sins I've ever committed and every one I ever might commit in the future?

Every one of them.

 Katie: I never knew that before. That is comforting to know—that He has already paid the price for me personally and knows what I am going through.

 Trevor: I never understood the Atonement that way either. I always just thought Jesus suffered a painful death on the cross and then was resurrected. I didn't understand all that He did for me personally.

And why did He do it for you?

 Katie: Because He wants to make us worthy for heaven. He wants us to be able to inherit the celestial kingdom.

Yes, he does, Katie. But what do you suppose His motivation is?

 **Katie:** Love?

That's right. A few years ago, President Gordon B. Hinckley told a story that illustrates the love Jesus has for each of us. He told of "'a one room school house in the mountains of Virginia where the boys were so rough no teacher had been able to handle them.

"'Then one day an inexperienced young teacher applied. He was told that every teacher had received an awful beating, but the teacher accepted the risk. The first day of school the teacher asked the boys to establish their own rules and the penalty for breaking the rules. The class came up with 10 rules, which were written on the blackboard. Then the teacher asked, "What shall we do with one who breaks the rules?"

"'"Beat him across the back ten times without his coat on," came the response.

"'A day or so later, . . . the lunch of a big student, named Tom, was stolen. "The thief was located—a little hungry fellow, about ten years old."

"'As Little Jim came up to take his licking, he pleaded to keep his coat on. "Take your coat off," the teacher said. "You helped make the rules!"

"The boy took off the coat. He had no shirt and revealed a bony little crippled body. As the teacher hesitated with the rod, Big Tom jumped to his feet and volunteered to take the boy's licking.

"'"Very well, there is a certain law that one can become a substitute for another. Are you all agreed?" the teacher asked.

"'After five strokes across Tom's back, the rod broke. The class was sobbing. "Little Jim had reached up and caught Tom with both arms around his neck. 'Tom, I'm sorry that I stole your lunch, but I was awful hungry. Tom, I will love you till I die for taking my licking for me! Yes, I will love you forever!'"'"[6]

President Hinckley then quoted Isaiah 53:4–5:

"Surely he hath borne *our* griefs, and carried *our* sorrows: . . .

" . . . he was wounded for *our* transgressions, he was bruised for *our* iniquities: the chastisement of *our* peace was upon him; and with *his* stripes *we* are healed" (emphasis added).

Jesus suffered the effects of every sin for every one of us so that we won't have to pay the price to justice ourselves if we will repent and come unto Him. His suffering for us was so intense that it caused Him "to tremble because of pain, and to bleed at every pore, and to suffer both body and spirit" (D&C 19:18). He overcame death for every one of us, so that every one of us will be resurrected. He felt every one of our individual sufferings, sicknesses, and physical and emotional pains simply so that He can know how to help us overcome our problems. In the words of President James E. Faust: "Because of the perfect atonement of Jesus, just men may be made perfect."[7] His perfect Atonement is what makes it possible for us to become perfected through Him and dwell in our Heavenly Father's presence in the celestial kingdom, pure and holy. How does that make you feel toward Him?

 Olivia: It makes me love Him more than I can say.

Me too. Me too.

CLASS #8

Amazing Grace

 Justin: You still haven't answered my question I asked earlier.

What question was that, Justin?

 Justin: I still don't get how Jesus being perfect makes me perfect. We just learned that Jesus suffered and paid the price for all of us, but I still don't get it.

Well, maybe a little activity will help you get it. Do you play basketball at all?

 Justin: No, not really. I'm a gamer more than a basketball player.

You'll be perfect then, no pun intended. Come up here and take this small foam basketball. All right, over against that wall I have a garbage can. I'm going to give you five shots, and I want to see how many you can make. If you make five for five, I'll give you this candy bar.

 Justin: I probably won't make any of them.

Just try your best, my man.

 Justin: [shoots and misses]

73

0 for 1 . . . you have four more shots . . .

 Justin: [shoots and misses]
[shoots and misses]

 Trevor: Come on, Justin, my grandma shoots better than that!

Easy, Trevor . . . you'll get your chance after Justin, so I wouldn't talk trash quite yet.

 Trevor: I'll hit five for five.

 Katie: Justin, just pretend that the hoop is Trevor's big mouth. That way it will seem so big you can't miss it.

 Justin: [shoots and makes it]

 Katie: There you go, Justin, nice shot.

 Justin: [shoots and makes it]

Good job, my friend. All right, you made two out of five. The good news is that you shoot just as well as most NBA centers do from the foul line. The bad news is that you didn't make five out of five, which was the requirement for the reward. You weren't perfect. If how well you just shot determined which eternal kingdom you will go to, what would you say you've earned? Where would you go, based on two for five?

 Trevor: [under his breath] Outer darkness.

 Mikayla: That's where you'll be going if you don't start being a little nicer, Trevor.

 Justin: I don't know. I think two for five would maybe get me to the terrestrial kingdom, the middle one.

On your own efforts, that sounds about right. Right in the middle. Not the five-for-five perfection that was required and which Trevor thinks he can do, but good enough to be in the middle. Speaking of Trevor, why don't you come on up and walk the walk instead of just talking the talk.

 Trevor: I'd love to. Let me show you how it's done. Try not to get too excited, ladies.

[shoots and makes it] That's what I'm talkin' about!

[shoots and makes it] Two for two.

[shoots and makes it] This is too easy.

 Dirk: Pride cometh before the fall, bro.

 Trevor: [shoots and makes it] Not this time. Here we go, five for five.

[shoots and misses it]

 Dirk: Told ya.

Okay. Nice shooting, Tex. You hit four out of five. You almost had the required five for five, but Dirk psyched you out a little and got in your head, so you don't get the reward. So, based on your performance, which kingdom would you go to?

 Trevor: Four for five is pretty good. I would say that's celestial shooting.

Four for five is pretty good, but it doesn't meet the requirement. Remember, no unclean thing can dwell with God. No imperfections. No misses. No sins. Even if you shot 99 out of 100, it still falls short of perfection. One A- forever ruins the 4.0. An eternal 3.99999999. Close enough, you are almost there, but still just a little short.

Trevor: So I have to go the terrestrial kingdom with Justin? That's pretty lame.

 Justin: Come visit me in my lowly station Mr. Five-for-Five-er.

Now, to be honest with you, what Trevor just said is true: it is actually pretty lame to expect that none of us will miss a shot. If you watch an average basketball game, everyone who plays misses a shot here or there. As a matter of fact, if you make only half the shots you take in a game you are a good shooter. The great Michael Jordan only had a career shooting percentage of 49.7 percent.[1] We are going to miss shots in the game of life. Each of us is going to fall short. Each of us is going to sin.

 Dirk: Teach, you're depressing me again.

It's depressing only if we forget our key scripture we read in D&C 76:69. Speaking of those who make it to the celestial kingdom, it says: "These are they who are just men *made perfect through Jesus* the mediator of the new covenant" (emphasis added). "Just men"—or in other words good people, or good shooters, in our analogy. Not perfect shooters, but good shooters made perfect through Jesus.

 Justin: I still don't get it.

Come up here again, Justin, and maybe you will. I want you to shoot five shots again and see how many you make.

 Justin: I thought my humiliation was over.

No, you're going to hit five for five, just watch.

 Justin: [shoots and misses, but the teacher rebounds it and puts it back in]

One for one.

 Justin: No, I missed it.

I know, but I rebounded it and put it back in. I cleaned up your miss. Shoot again, I'm ready for you.

 Justin: [shoots and makes it]

Two for two . . . perfection on its way.

 Justin: [shoots and misses, but the teacher grabs it and sticks it in the hoop again]

Three for three.

 Justin: [shoots and makes it]

One more, brother, and perfection is there . . .

 Justin: [shoots and misses it, but the teacher puts it back in again]

Beautiful, my man! Five for five!

 Justin: But I wasn't five for five, I was two for five again.

No, all five shots got put in the basket. You see, with Jesus, you have the perfect teammate, the perfect rebounder, who is ready, able, and waiting to put back all your misses. As long as you are trying your hardest to make that shot, even if you brick it off the top of the backboard, the Savior will clean it up if you miss, and put it back in. This is what we sometimes refer to in the Church as *grace*. Your shooting, plus Jesus' rebounding, equals perfection. Your best efforts plus Jesus' perfect Atonement equals a perfectly purified celestial person. Even if you're zero for five, as long as you are giving it your best, Christ's perfect Atonement can make you five for five with no misses and no sins. This is what "grace" is. Make sense?

 Katie: Is this the same kind of grace in the song "Amazing Grace"?

Yes, it is, and how sweet the sound of it! The scriptures are full of references to God's grace saving us. In the New Testament the Apostle Paul talks a lot about grace. One of his most famous statements on grace is in Ephesians 2:8-9. In it Paul teaches:

"For by grace are ye saved through faith; and that not of yourselves: it is the gift of God:

"Not of works, lest any man should boast."

In other words, Paul is saying that one of the greatest gifts God has given the world is the saving grace of Jesus Christ. His grace can save us and make us perfect. "Not of works" means that Paul understands that none of us, on our own, can qualify for the perfection of the celestial kingdom. None of us can live a life without sin. None of us will shoot ten thousand for ten thousand without a single missed shot in our lives. Let's read what the Bible Dictionary teaches us about grace before we go on. Katie, will you read that for us?

 Katie: Sure.

As Katie reads I want you to look for any key phrases or words about grace that relate to our analogy. Go ahead, Katie.

 Katie: The Bible Dictionary says: "The main idea of the word is divine means of help or strength, given through the bounteous mercy and love of Jesus Christ.

"It is through the grace of the Lord Jesus, made possible by his atoning sacrifice, that mankind will be raised in immortality, every person receiving his body from the grave in a condition of everlasting life. It is likewise through the grace of the Lord that individuals, through faith in the atonement of Jesus Christ and repentance of their sins, receive strength and assistance to do good works that they otherwise would not be able to maintain if left to their own means. This grace is an enabling power that allows men and women to lay hold on eternal life and exaltation after they have expended their own best efforts."[2]

That's good to there. All right, what words or phrases jumped out to you?

Lindsay: I liked where it said it is "divine help or strength," like an extra boost beyond what I can do on my own.

Justin: There is another phrase in there that made me think of the basketball analogy. It's the one that says that by grace we "receive strength and assistance," kind of like how you were assisting me by rebounding my missed shots.

Mikayla: Yeah, I liked where it says that grace is an "enabling power."

Why do you like that phrase, Mikayla?

Mikayla: Because I've always felt like God has helped me do things, to be better than who I could be on my own by myself. Like, I pray a lot that He will help me in school and cheerleading and just to be a better person and choose the right, and I feel like He does help me be better. But I never knew that Him helping me like that was called "grace."

That is a great comment, Mikayla. God helping us be better in any way, shape, or form is part of being "saved by grace," whether He is helping us with an everyday need, like overcoming a bad habit or being more kind to others, or with an eternal need, such as resurrecting us. It is all part of being saved by grace. This is an important point to clearly understand: Grace not only cleans up our missed shots and makes us perfect, but it helps us be a better "shooter" so we do better in the game of life. Grace is an "enabling power" that also helps us give our "best efforts"—it helps us be better in all we do and is the power behind any good that we do.

 Trevor: So grace helps me be better at things I do, even things like football?

Yes, it does. Through God's grace He gave you the ability to live and breathe. Through God's grace He gave you your natural gifts and abilities and strengths. Through His grace He sent you to a family and situation where those abilities could be enhanced and developed through the opportunities He provided you. By grace God can help you maximize your gifts and abilities; He will help you become strong where you are weak. The *For the Strength of Youth* pamphlet teaches that "the Lord will make much more out of your life than you can by yourself. He will increase your opportunities, expand your vision, and strengthen you."[3] That is grace in action, and it can apply to all of us in all that we do. God's grace will help Justin get along with his mom, Katie be a better student, Mikayla in her cheerleading, David with his quorum responsibilities, Dirk in his desire to serve a mission, Olivia with her writing, and Lindsay with her friends. God's grace can literally help perfect us day by day, not just sin by sin.

 Lindsay: Yeah, when I was a little younger, I used to hear the hymn "I Need Thee Every Hour"[4] and think, "No, I don't. I don't need Jesus every *hour*. I need him when I repent, but I don't mess up and need repenting every hour. And I'll need Him when I die, but that'll be a long time away. So I don't need Him every hour. But then, as I became a teenager and started to face some tough situations—bad friends and boys and family things—I started realizing I needed God's help to fix things and overcome problems and I couldn't do it on my own. I would pray every day that God would give me the strength to face and overcome my struggles. I was tellin' my grandma about it one day, and she told me that what I needed was Jesus' grace to strengthen and bless and help me. So I started to pray for strength, every day, and He helped me. I've learned that I don't need Jesus just to repent, but that I also need Jesus to strengthen me so I don't need to repent as much. I've started to feel like I need Jesus' grace all the time. It makes me want to change the name of the hymn now to "I Need Thee Every Second," because that is more like what it is for me.

Lindsay, that is a great example of what grace does and what it is. Grace doesn't just sweep in and appear at the last minute and save us—as we sometimes think—but it helps us all along our journey in life by giving us increased strength and abilities each day, especially where we are weak (see Ether 12:27).

 David: So we do believe in being saved by grace, then? I always thought that was just a mainstream Christian thing.

It is a "Christian" thing, and Latter-day Saints are definitely Christian. Let's look at our own Book of Mormon and read some of its verses on grace. For example, look at 2 Nephi 2:8. Olivia, will you read that one?

 Olivia: "There is no flesh that can dwell in the presence of God, save it be through the merits, and mercy, and grace of the Holy Messiah."

Let's jump to 2 Nephi 10:24.

Dirk: I'll read that one: "It is only in and through the grace of God that ye are saved."

The most classic verse on grace in the Book of Mormon is Nephi's amazing statement in 2 Nephi 25:23. Make sure you have this highlighted: "For we know that it is by grace that we are saved, after all we can do." There are two ways to read this statement:

a) We are saved by grace only after we have done our very best (including relying on the Lord to help us do our very best), and

b) Even after all we do in righteousness, we still cannot save ourselves. No matter how much good we do, it will not be enough, and we will still need to be saved by grace.

 David: So which reading is right?

I think they both are. No matter what, none of us can save ourselves, and grace requires our best efforts to qualify for it. Thankfully, the Lord helps us be able to give our best efforts.

And if you think that verse on grace is cool, let's read the best one of all. For a moment, pretend that you are Moroni and you are writing the concluding chapter of the Book of Mormon—a book that will be read by millions and millions the world over for hundreds of years. A book that will testify to the world of the truthfulness of Joseph Smith's prophetic calling, the restored Church on the earth, and above all, the reality of the Atonement of Jesus Christ. How would you end the book? What would your final message to the world be? Well, let's see how Moroni sums up the message of the book of books. Go to Moroni 10:32 and read it on your own:

"Yea, come unto Christ, and *be perfected in him,* and deny yourselves of all ungodliness; and if ye shall deny yourselves of all ungodliness, and love God with all your might, mind and strength, then is his grace sufficient for you, that *by his grace ye may be perfect in Christ;* and if by the grace of God ye are perfect in Christ, ye can in nowise deny the power of God" (emphasis added).

What a way to end the Book of Mormon! Moroni's final message is all about how we will be made perfect by the grace of Jesus Christ and His perfect Atonement. We don't need to try to be perfect by ourselves because Jesus will make us perfect. Come unto Christ and *be perfected in Him*! Why do you think He chose to end the book that way?

David: Because that is the main message of the gospel: Christ will save us if we come unto Him.

Katie: Yeah, but don't we have to qualify for Christ's grace to save us? I mean, Moroni qualified it in those verses by saying we need to "deny" ourselves of "ungodliness" and "love God," and "*then* is his grace sufficient for you." I understand that you are saying that Christ's grace can save us and make us perfect, but He won't do that for everyone. He won't perfect everyone. It looks like He does it only for people who qualify for His grace.

Great point, Katie. Yes, we do need to qualify for some of God's grace, and I will tell you how we specifically do that next class. But remember, Christ's saving grace is individually tailored to the dimensions of each of our lives.

Katie: What do you mean?

Well, look at some of the Savior's parables, such as the parable of the laborers in Matthew 20:1–16. In that parable, the Lord hires servants for the payment of a penny a day. When the day is part over, he hires more laborers for a penny a day, even though they will work fewer hours. And when the last hour of the day comes around, he sees some people standing idly by and also hires them to work for him for a penny. Whether you work all day, half the day, or for an hour of the day, he rewards all the same. Whether you are a lifelong member, or converted at thirty-five, or were baptized at ninety-nine and died the next day, God rewards all with His grace and pays them equally with celestial reward, regardless of how long they may have served.

Lindsay: Isn't there another parable like that, about talents or something?

Yes, there is, the parable of the talents in Matthew 25:14–30. Do you know it well enough to summarize it, Lindsay?

 Lindsay: I think in that one Jesus gives everyone talents, except they are different amounts. I think he gives one person five talents, one person two, and another person one.

Exactly, and what happens?

 Lindsay: Well, the person with five talents uses them and earns five more, and the person with two talents does the same. But the person with one talent doesn't do anything, and the Lord takes it away from him.

Good summary. What is interesting is to look in verse 21 at the reward of the person who earned ten total talents, and in verse 23 at the reward of the person who only earned four total talents. Even though one person almost doubled the other, what was the reward?

 Mikayla: That's crazy. They are the exact same thing, almost word for word. It says they both enter "into the joy of [the] Lord."

So does God care if you are a ten-talent member or a four-talent member?

 Mikayla: No, He primarily cares that you do your best with what you are given.

Exactly. God's grace will perfect the six-talent member just as much and just as perfectly as the ten-talent member. What about the one-talent member?

 David: Well, in verses 26 through 29 the Lord rebukes him for not doing anything and casts him out.

Did He cast him out because he had only one talent, or because he didn't do anything?

 David: Because he buried it and didn't do anything with it.

Do you think it is fair to assume, based on the other two people with talents in the parable, that the Lord would have given the one-talent member an equal reward if he had brought back another talent, making him a two-talent member?

 David: I think so.

So do I. I think God will judge and reward us based on our own individual efforts, regardless of others' efforts. He won't compare us. That is why in the parable of the sower, the Lord cares only that the seed was received by "good ground." He didn't care how much fruit each seed produced, "some an hundredfold, some sixtyfold, some thirtyfold" (Matthew 13:8), as long as they brought forth something of their efforts. It appears that there isn't a generic bar, halfway up the perfection scale, that we all need to attain before God's grace kicks in and perfects us. We are all different, with different potentials and capacities, and God's grace takes that into consideration.

I realized this truth one day when my wife came home with our van full of groceries to be carried in. I went out, and to prove to my wife how strong I am, I loaded up both my arms—past my elbows—with about a dozen grocery sacks and a gallon of milk in each hand. My little girl Jane, who was about three at the time, came out to help, too, and just as I was walking in with my two gallons of milk and dozen plastic grocery sacks, I noticed her struggling to pick up and carry one single, solitary gallon of milk. It seemed it was half her size and weight. She could barely do it, but she flopped and dropped and eventually plopped it inside. Now my question is: who worked harder?

Lindsay: Your girl did, that's for sure.

Even though I carried twenty times as much? I did twenty times more work!

Trevor: But you have a hundred times more strength than she does.

Exactly. And if God's requirement for the celestial grocery sack carrying contest was one hundred items, and I came in, arms loaded with fourteen items, and my daughter with only one, guess what?

Trevor: You would receive the same reward.

Yes, we would. Christ's grace would make up for the eighty-five grocery items that I lack, and the ninety-nine that my daughter lacked. But the key is that we were both trying our hardest. We were both giving our "own best efforts"[5] that would have qualified us for Christ's grace. Jump back to the Bible Dictionary, page 697, and read in the last paragraph:

"Grace cannot suffice without *total effort* on the part of the recipient. Hence the explanation, 'It is by grace that we are saved, *after all we can do*' (2 Nephi 25:23)" (emphasis added).

Dirk: So I can't just intentionally miss the shot—close my eyes and air-ball it just because I know Jesus will pick up the slack.

No, you can't—you have to *try* to make the shot, Dirk. You cannot intentionally miss, intentionally sin, and expect that Christ and His grace will just clean up the mess because of His infinite goodness. No, you would get benched by the coach if you did that. You would be off the court of grace.

Justin: But He doesn't care if we are two for five or four for five, as long as we are trying. He'll still rebound our misses and put them back in and make us perfect shooters, right?

Right. His grace gives us the ability to shoot well and cleans up our misses. We'll be perfect celestial shooters because of His grace, as long as we are trying our best to make the shot. As long as we stay "valiant" in our efforts.

Trevor: Man, I want Jesus on my team. I'd never lose.

No, you definitely wouldn't. And you just said something really important—more important than you probably think.

Trevor: I did? What? That I'd never lose? I wasn't being prideful this time, just stating the facts.

No, not that you'd never lose. It was the comment about your teammate. You said you wanted Jesus on *your* team. But you'll never lose as long as you are on *Christ's* team. The key is being on Christ's team.

CLASS #9

Joined with Jesus

 Trevor: So I've been thinking about what you said last class. Jesus has a team?

Metaphorically speaking, yes, He does. The most important thing we can do in this game of life is to make sure we are on Christ's team, that we are wearing the same color jersey as He is and, most importantly, that we have His team name across the front of it. Lindsay, I know you play sports. Aren't you on the school's volleyball team?

 Lindsay: Uh-huh, and basketball team, too.

How did you get on those teams?

 Lindsay: Well, I went to tryouts and played, and, I don't know, the coach liked me, I guess, and put me on the team.

I would assume that the coach picked you because you had certain abilities, certain qualities that he or she was looking for, right? Such as the ability to serve well, make a good pass, or spike it. And also other things such as your attitude and potential to be a good teammate.

 Lindsay: Yeah, I guess so.

So back to our teammate analogy with Christ: If the key to

qualifying for Christ's grace is to be on His team, how do we "make the cut" so to speak? What abilities and qualities do we have to show to get on His team and have His name on our team jersey? How do we join the same team as Jesus?

 Mikayla: Well, we have to believe in Him as the Son of God and love Him.

Good answer, Mikayla. Believing in Jesus and loving Him are critical first steps. But does saying we believe in Him and love Him automatically put us on Christ's team? After all, saying that I love basketball and believing it is a good sport doesn't get me on the school team.

 Mikayla: That's true.

Simply believing in Jesus can't be enough. The book of James teaches us that "the devils also believe, and tremble" (James 2:19). There has to be something we *do* that gets us on Christ's team. Now, before we go on here, I want to make one thing absolutely clear one more time for all of us—we cannot save ourselves. We cannot do anything that on our own will save us. Only by the grace of Christ are we saved, just as we discussed.

 Katie: Why do you feel like you have to make that clear? I mean, I think we get it that it is only Jesus who can save us.

Let me tell you why I want to make that clear. Sometimes Latter-day Saints are accused of thinking that we can save ourselves through our own works. In other words, if I can just attend enough church meetings, read my scriptures for so many hours, say so many prayers, bake a few dozen cookies for the neighbors, set up a few thousand metal chairs, and do enough temple service, then I will *earn* my way into heaven. Some of us might mistakenly think that *our works,* not Jesus' works, will save us.

David: Well, doesn't doing good things like that qualify us for heaven, though? Isn't that kind of what we have been reading about in D&C 76—the things we need to do that qualify us for the celestial kingdom?

No, we haven't. We haven't been studying the things *we* need to do that will qualify us for the celestial kingdom. We can't qualify ourselves for the celestial kingdom, not at all.

 Justin: Well, then, what have we been studying this whole time? I thought the whole point of this was to figure out what we need to do to qualify for the celestial kingdom.

No, what we have been studying are the things that will *qualify us for Christ's atoning grace.* There is a difference. It doesn't matter how much tithing we pay, how much service we give, how many righteous things we do—we cannot and will not save ourselves through our own works and our own goodness. King Benjamin in the Book of Mormon taught that "if ye should serve [God] with all your whole souls yet ye would be unprofitable servants" (Mosiah 2:21). We can't qualify ourselves for salvation—*we can only qualify ourselves for Christ's grace, and then Christ will bring us to the celestial kingdom through His grace.* King Benjamin also taught that our *good works seal us to Christ,* so "that [we] may be *brought* to heaven" (Mosiah 5:15; emphasis added) by Jesus. Alma the Younger had it right when he reminded his own son "that there is no other way or means whereby man can be saved, only in and through Christ" (Alma 38:9).

 Olivia: I think I get it. So the requirements we read about in section 76—faith in Jesus Christ, repentance, baptism, and receiving the Holy Ghost, don't qualify us for heaven—they are what qualify us to be Christ's people.

Exactly! That is one of the most sublime truths of the gospel: Our good works don't perfect us; but they do qualify us for Christ's perfecting Atonement. So, back to the question I asked a minute ago with the basketball analogy: What must we *do* to get on Christ's team? How do we get His name on our jersey so He can carry us to the victory? How do we take His name upon us?

Lindsay: I get it. I get it. We do it through baptism, don't we? Don't we take His name on us when we get baptized and become His disciples?

That's right! You see, what our good works do is qualify us to make *covenants* with Christ, to be linked, or joined with Him—to get on His celestial side. If we can qualify ourselves to make covenants with God, and if we are true to those covenants, then Christ will perfect us. If we claim Christ's name on us through covenant, then at the final judgment Christ will claim our names on Him. Make sense?

Lindsay: It makes perfect sense to me . . .

Katie: So I guess that is why the Church is so concerned with baptizing other people and getting more converts. My boyfriend isn't a member of the Church, or a member of any church, for that matter. He is always saying that you don't really need organized religion or to be baptized as long as you are an ethical, thoughtful, open-minded person. He thinks the only reason that the LDS Church wants to baptize people is so that the Church can make money off their tithing and become more powerful in political influence. But now that we are talking about it, it makes a lot more sense to me why we do need an organized Church. If it is all about making covenants, then I guess we need to know who truly has authority to perform the ordinances and who is worthy to make covenants. And it takes an organized Church of Jesus Christ to do that.

Good insights, Katie. In essence, that is why the Church exists: to provide the priesthood covenants and ordinances that connect us to Christ so He can save and exalt God's children. Let's do a little searching activity and find some scriptures where Jesus teaches that it is the connection to Him *by covenant* that is the key to salvation. Take a minute to see what you can find.

Justin: Well, here's one. This is from the sacrament prayer in Moroni 4:3. It says that those who take the sacrament "are willing to take upon them the name of thy Son . . ." So that covenant is connected to taking Jesus' name on us.

You are right. As we partake of the sacrament we renew our baptismal covenant to take Christ's name upon ourselves. We'll talk more about the sacrament in a minute. What other examples did you find?

Trevor: Hey, listen to these verses I just found. They are exactly what we are talking about. I think—well, the chapter heading says it anyway—that this is when King Benjamin just got done talking from on top of the tower to all his people. Listen to what King Benjamin says. I'm in Mosiah 5:7–9:

"And now, because of the covenant which ye have made *ye shall be called the children of Christ,* his sons, and his daughters; . . .

"And under this head ye are made free, and there is no other head whereby ye can be made free. There is no other name given whereby salvation cometh; therefore, I would that ye should take upon you the name of Christ, all you that have entered into the covenant with God that ye should be obedient unto the end of your lives.

"And it shall come to pass that whosoever doeth this shall be found at the right hand of God, for he shall know the name by which he is called; for he shall be called by the name of Christ" (emphasis added).

So what truths about covenants do you see taught in those verses, Trevor?

Trevor: Well, that if we make a covenant with Christ, then we take His name on us and we become kind of like His own children, like His family. And if we do that, then at the last day Christ will say, "Yeah, he's with me. He's part of my family," and save us. That is awesome.

Well said, Trevor. This same doctrine is taught in the parable of the ten virgins. The five who were foolish tried to get the Lord to open the celestial door for them—to allow them to be part of Christ's celestial family, too—"But he answered and said, Verily I say unto you, *I know you not*" (Matthew 25:12; emphasis added).

Mikayla: Here is another verse about covenants that I found. This one is in the New Testament. It is when Jesus is telling his apostles to go out and teach the whole world. He says in Mark 16:16: "He that believeth and is baptized shall be saved; but he that believeth not shall be damned." So it's like Jesus is saying, "It isn't enough just to believe in me. You need to make a covenant with me. You need to get baptized."

That is a great verse, Mikayla. As a matter of fact, that phrase, to believe *and* be baptized, is one of the most oft-repeated phrases in the scriptures about being saved. Look at all these verses that say almost the same thing, word for word:

"And he commandeth all men that they must repent, and be baptized in his name, having perfect faith in the Holy One of Israel, or they cannot be saved in the kingdom of God" (2 Nephi 9:23).

"And whosoever will hearken unto my words and repenteth and is baptized, the same shall be saved" (3 Nephi 23:5).

"And whoso believeth in me, and is baptized, the same shall be saved; and they are they who shall inherit the kingdom of God.

"And whoso believeth not in me, and is not baptized, shall be damned" (3 Nephi 11:33–34).

"And he hath said: Repent all ye ends of the earth, and come unto me, and be baptized in my name, and have faith in me, that ye may be saved" (Moroni 7:34).

"And he that believeth and is baptized shall be saved, but he that believeth not shall be damned" (Mormon 9:23; this verse is repeated almost word for word in D&C 68:9; D&C 112:29; and in Ether 4:18).

This idea of making covenants with Christ and being saved *because of the covenants* is everywhere in the scriptures, all the way back through the Old Testament. You remember when Moses is trying to convince Pharaoh to let the children of Israel go free from slavery? Pharaoh won't let them go, so God sends a number of plagues to punish the Egyptians, plagues such as boils and frogs and flies. The last plague God sends is the destroying angel, to kill all of the firstborn males in the land of Egypt.

 Dirk: Ah, yeah, man . . . that cartoon movie of that is awesome. With the breathing, floating, white misty stuff sucking the life out of people in the middle of the night.

Why did the children of Israel's firstborn children not die? Do you remember?

 Katie: Didn't they kill a lamb and put its blood on the doorpost, and when the destroying angel saw the blood of the lamb it would pass by them and not kill them? That is where the Jews started the whole Passover meal, wasn't it?

Exactly. And what did killing the lamb and its blood symbolize?

 David: It symbolized the Atonement of Christ. Him spilling His blood and saving us from the things that destroy us, like sin and death.

Yes. Exodus 12:5–6 tells us that the lamb had to be without blemish, a male, and that the children of Israel were to kill it in the evening. Who does that sound like?

Trevor: That sounds a lot like Jesus, because He was all those things. One of His names is the Lamb of God. And He was the Firstborn of the Father, without any sin, and the nation of Israel had Him killed in the evening. That is crazy how all that matches up.

It's supposed to, because the Passover lamb symbolizes Jesus and His atoning sacrifice. But look what the Lord says in Exodus 12:13 about the blood of the lamb. Justin, will you read that?

Justin: "And the blood shall be to you for a token upon the houses where ye are: and when I see the blood, I will pass over you, and the plague shall not be upon you to destroy you, when I smite the land of Egypt."

What do you think that means, "the blood shall be to you for a token"?

Lindsay: I think it means like it is proof, ya know? Like, hey, we here at this house believe in your word and did what you said.

Actually, *proof* is another word for a token. Other words the thesaurus uses for "token" are words such as *symbol* and *gesture* and *sign*. What is the symbol, gesture, sign, or token the Lord asks his believers to do in our day to be saved by Him?

David: From all those verses we just looked at and from section 76, the sign is baptism.

That's right, David. Elder D. Todd Christofferson said, "By [the] ordinance [of baptism] we become part of the covenant people of the Lord and heirs of the celestial kingdom of God."[1] So the children of Israel were saved from the destroying angel because of the token, or sign, they had placed on their doors with the blood of the lamb, and today we are saved by the sign and covenant token of baptism. Let's look at one other cool story in the Old Testament about covenants saving people. Go figure—it also involves more death and covenants.

 Justin: What good Old Testament story doesn't involve death?

 Katie: Like, none of them.

The children of Israel were heading back to the promised land, and God told them to wipe out all the people who had taken their land and started living in it while they were away as slaves in Egypt.

 Justin: Nice, more Old Testament fighting.

Well, not for one woman named Rahab. She was *not* an Israelite and was one of the people who was about to be wiped out. However, she knew that the Israelites were God's people, and so she decided to help two Israelite spies escape safely and avoid harm from her people. To repay her, the Israelite spies promised that when they attacked the city, they would not hurt her or any in her house. Rahab asked the Israelite spies to "give me a true *token*" (Joshua 2:12; emphasis added) that they would save her alive. Let's read what the spies said and see if you can see the symbolism in their covenant. David, will you read what the spies said in Joshua 2:18 and what Rahab said in verse 21?

 David: Yeah, I'd be glad to. It says,

"Behold, when we come into the land, thou shalt bind this line of scarlet thread in the window which thou didst let us down by: and thou shalt bring thy father, and thy mother, and thy brethren, and all thy father's household, home unto thee. . . .

"And she said, According unto your words, so be it. And she sent them away, and they departed: and she bound the scarlet line in the window."

Now, what do you notice that is symbolic about covenants in this story?

 David: Well, she asked for a "token" like we talked about, or a sign, or agreement. I think it is interesting that the token was a scarlet thread in the window.

Why is that interesting to you?

 David: Well, because of the symbolic color of blood—like the blood of the Atonement again. It is similar to the Passover story we just read. When the soldiers see the red on the house—the token that is symbolic of the Atonement—they don't hurt the person in that house and they are saved. It's pretty cool how Rahab's story and the Passover story are almost exactly the same.

It is pretty cool, and so is this: Let's look at one more symbolic thing about the story in Joshua 6:25. It says, "And Joshua saved Rahab the harlot alive, and her father's household, and all that she had; and she dwelleth in Israel even unto this day."

 David: Yeah . . . what's so cool about that?

Well, another interesting thing about the analogy of Rahab's covenant and scarlet thread is why Joshua saved her. What does the name *Joshua* mean? If you take a look at the Bible Dictionary, page 718, it tells us that another name for Joshua is . . .

Mikayla: Jesus. I know that because my little brother is named Joshua and my dad is always reminding him that Joshua is another way of saying the name Jesus.

 David: That's pretty cool if you read the verse with Jesus' name instead of Joshua. The verse would say that Jesus saved her because of the covenant she made, and the red scarlet thread that is the token of that covenant.

It is cool. And we could go on and on and on about different scriptural stories where good people made covenants, and how the covenants are what saved them. Think of the story of Captain Moroni and the title of liberty in the Book of Mormon. His people were about ready to be killed by Amalickiah, who wanted all the glory and power of being a king and to take away their freedom and their lives. Who does that sound like?

 David: Lucifer?

It sure does. So Moroni takes his coat, rends it, or in other words rips or tears it, and writes on it, "In memory of our God" (Alma 46:12), and lifts it up for all who are believers in Christ to see. He says, "Behold, whosoever will maintain this title upon the land, let them come forth in the strength of the Lord, and enter into a covenant that they will maintain their rights, and their religion, that the Lord God may bless them" (Alma 46:20).

Then all the people come running together, "rending their garments in *token,* or as a covenant, that they would not forsake the Lord their God" (Alma 46:21; emphasis added). All those who enter into the covenant are saved, and those who don't enter into the covenant are "put to death" (vs. 35).

 Trevor: That story of the title of liberty is one of my favorites in all the scriptures. I never realized that part of it could be symbolic about how covenants save us. Even the name of the coat that Captain Moroni tore and wrote on, the title of liberty, could be symbolic. Maybe it isn't just talking about physical freedom but spiritual freedom as well.

It very well could be. That is a great insight. You see, the key principle from all of these stories is the need to be *connected with Christ*. The only way we connect ourselves to Christ is through covenants, through taking His name on us in some sort of token, or sign, or gesture. If we do that, He will save us, just as He saved the Israelites and Rahab and Captain Moroni's people. Elder Christofferson said that "our access to [God's] power is through our covenants with Him. . . . In these divine agreements, God binds himself to sustain, sanctify, and exalt us in return for our commitment to serve Him."[2]

For those of you in the class who are math gurus, this analogy might help you see the saving power of covenants more clearly: What does this mathematical sign mean?

 Mikayla: It is the symbol for infinity.

Right. And what does infinity mean in mathematical or conceptual terms?

 Mikayla: Well, it means you can't put a number to it because it is limitless. You can't take away from it, and you can't add to it. It has no beginning and no end. That is why it is written as a continuous loop.

 Trevor: Pretty impressive for a cheerleader.

Excellent summary from our new resident math genius, Mikayla. Now take a look at 2 Nephi 9:7 and notice the key word that Jacob uses to describe the Atonement of Jesus Christ.

"Wherefore, it must needs be an infinite atonement—save it

should be an infinite atonement this corruption could not put on incorruption."

 Olivia: He calls it an "infinite atonement."

We know Jesus' Atonement was a *perfect* Atonement, but why do you think Jacob calls it an "infinite" Atonement? What does that mean according to the definition of infinity that Mikayla just gave us?

 Olivia: Well, I think it means that Jesus' Atonement has no limits to it. He can save as many people as come unto Him and follow Him.

He can, Olivia, you are right. But here is where the key to that infinite Atonement comes in. Let's do some math equations.

 Justin: Really? I thought this was seminary, not math. I come here so I don't have to do things like economics, basketball, and math. So far we've done all three in these lessons.

This is the kind of math that is spiritually good for you, Justin. All right, solve this equation:

$$\infty + 30 =$$

 Dirk: Thirty-infinity. Yeah, bro. Dirk . . . the new resident math genius.

 Mikayla: The answer is just infinity. Sorry, Dirk. You can't add to infinity. It already exists as a limitless number.

 Dirk: I knew there was a reason I didn't take calculus. All right, take away my short-lived math genius title I just earned.

All right, how about this one:

$$\infty + 60 =$$

Dirk: Infinity-sixty! Just kidding . . . don't think I'm that slow in the noggin. It would be infinity.

You're right, Dirk, it would still be infinity. One last one:

$$\infty + 100 =$$

Lindsay: Infinity.

Good. Unfortunately, I'm not testing math skills. I'm testing gospel understanding. So, what does this have to do with the Atonement, and more precisely, with covenants? What does this equation mean from a heavenly perspective?

David: Well, if Jacob said that Christ's Atonement is an infinite Atonement, then the infinity symbol means the Atonement.

So there is Christ in the equation, and where are we?

Katie: We would be the number. And the number would be symbolic of our good works we do here. We would be the 30, or 60, or 100.

Yes, we would. And just as in the parable of the sower—"some an hundredfold, some sixtyfold, some thirtyfold" (Matthew 13:8)—we all will be on differing levels of righteousness when we die, based on our individual mortal situations, but the equation still comes out the same.

Trevor: So in the equation, the equal sign means that we will get into heaven then, right? We all end up as infinity.

Or another way to say it is we all end up *perfect* or *perfected*. But what is the key to the equation? What is it that joins our works of thirty with infinity? What does the plus symbol mean?

 Lindsay: It means we've made covenants, like we've been talking about. It means we are joined or connected with Jesus. And because we are joined with Jesus, He makes us perfect.

Beautiful, Lindsay! "Joined with Jesus"—that is a catchy phrase we should remember. Here is what the equation looks like if we write it out:

JESUS' INFINITE ATONEMENT (∞) PLUS COVENANTS (+) PLUS OUR GOOD WORKS (30, 60, 100) EQUALS (=) PERFECTION

So what does all of this talk about covenants mean to you guys?

 Lindsay: It means I want to do like the Young Women theme says. I want to make and keep sacred covenants.

When can you qualify for, make, and keep more covenants, since covenants are the key?

 Olivia: Each week when we take the sacrament, we renew our baptismal covenant to take the name of Christ on us again, don't we?

 David: And for the young men, we make a covenant with Christ when we receive the priesthood, like it says in the scripture mastery in D&C 84:33–39.

Great answers, Olivia and David. Any other times when we can make additional covenants, and become "joined with Jesus" as Lindsay said?

Katie: When we go to the temple. Don't we make more covenants there?

Yes. In the temple is where we make the most sacred and solemn covenants—the covenants that will eventually *exalt* us in the celestial kingdom. Actually, Elder David A. Bednar explained that it is only through the temple ordinances that we can *ultimately and completely* take upon us the name of Christ.[3] You see, our lives should be a continual cycle of qualifying for, making, and keeping sacred covenants. The more we live what I call the "righteous cycle" of covenants, the more connected to Christ through covenant we will be, thus assuring ourselves that we will be perfected by Him and qualify for the celestial kingdom.

 Justin: The righteous cycle? What is the righteous cycle?

 Dirk: It sounds like a sweet new brand of mountain bikes.

No, Dirk, the "righteous cycle" isn't a brand of bikes—it is what the scriptures call "enduring to the end" or being "valiant" in our testimony of Jesus (see D&C 18:22; D&C 76:79). It is the opposite of the pride cycle in the Book of Mormon. It is the key to qualifying for, making, and keeping the covenants that allows Jesus to save us in the celestial kingdom. It is what we should do every week of our lives. And that is where we'll pick up next class.

CLASS #10

The Righteous Cycle

Let's begin learning about the "righteous cycle" by asking one question: How many of you wish you could get rebaptized right now? How many of you wish that, although it was nice to be baptized when you were eight years old, you could have a fresh start today now that you are sixteen or seventeen? I mean, the worst thing most us had done by the age of eight was tell a little lie to our parents or maybe kick one of our siblings in the shin. But now? Now that you are teenagers and growing up and really faced with temptation and, unfortunately, have made some real mistakes?

 Mikayla: I have thought that before. I have always been a little jealous of people like Olivia who were baptized when they were older and could have all their previous mistakes of their teenage years washed away.

What if I told you, Mikayla, that you could get rebaptized this week, and that you could start just as fresh and clean right now as you did when you were a kid? Would you like that?

 Mikayla: Are you kidding? I would love that. I think we all would. Who wouldn't want to start over?

Well, the good news is that you can. All of us can. As a matter of fact, if things are right in our lives, we can get "baptized again" this

104

Sunday. And the Sunday after that, and the Sunday after that, for the rest of our lives.

 Katie: Are you talking about taking the sacrament?

Yes, I am.

 Katie: I thought that taking the sacrament was just a renewal of the covenants we made at baptism, not a new cleansing of us from sin.

It's both. Partaking of the sacrament renews our baptismal covenants and reconnects us to Christ, *and* it cleanses us from sin when taken in the right way. Let's read what Elder Dallin H. Oaks taught: "We are commanded to repent of our sins and to come to the Lord with a broken heart and a contrite spirit and partake of the sacrament in compliance with its covenants. *When we renew our baptismal covenants in this way, the Lord renews the cleansing effect of our baptism.* In this way we are made clean and can always have His Spirit to be with us."[1]

Let's read one more from President Boyd K. Packer. Katie, will you read that one?

 Katie: "Generally we understand that, conditioned upon repentance, the ordinance of baptism washes our sins away. Some wonder if they were baptized too soon. If only they could be baptized now and have a clean start. But that is not necessary! Through the ordinance of the sacrament, you renew the covenants made at baptism. When you meet all of the conditions of repentance, however difficult, you may be forgiven and your transgressions will trouble your mind no more."[2]

You see, we weren't baptized too soon when we were eight. That is when we start to become accountable for our sins according to the scriptures (see D&C 68:25–27). Our baptism at age eight makes it possible to be cleansed from the sins we might commit from that point on. In His mercy, the Lord has made it possible for us to be cleansed again and again, each week, from the moment we are baptized, whether we are eight or eighteen or eighty.

 Justin: So you're telling me that I can be totally forgiven of all my sins this Sunday and be totally clean like I was when I was eight, if I take the sacrament? That blows my mind.

Yes, you can! Elder Jeffrey R. Holland said, "Think for a moment how different our lives could be if through repentance we were made clean each and every Sabbath and could start each week absolutely pure, renewed, refreshed—totally confident of our standing before God."[3]

 Justin: So every week I can be forgiven?

Yes, it is possible every week. That is why it is so important that we attend sacrament meeting each week and partake of the sacrament. This could be why President Joseph Fielding Smith called sacrament meeting "the most important meeting which we have."[4] When I was on my mission, we baptized a very old woman who was literally on her death bed. She wanted to be baptized so badly before she died. So, after teaching her the gospel and with her family's permission, we carried her out of her bed, laid her down in the backseat of a car, drove her to the church, and carried her down into the baptismal font. She was baptized by two elders who held her horizontally and then lowered her under the water. When she came up out of the water, she just kept saying, "Thank you, elders, thank you," over and over again. We confirmed her that day a member of the Church. She died a week later.

 Trevor: Really? That is amazing. Straight to heaven for her!

That is what I thought, also. How lucky she was to have exercised faith, repented, been baptized, received the Holy Ghost, and been cleansed from sin within a week of her death! But then it dawned on me: we can all do the same. We can all exercise faith, repent, renew our baptismal covenant, and receive the Holy Ghost within roughly a week of our death through the sacred ordinance of the sacrament. That is one of the reasons why the Lord commanded us to take the sacrament *each week* on the Sabbath day (see D&C 59:9). What would happen if I were renewing my covenants with Christ only once a year, or once every ten years, or not at all?

David: Then you probably wouldn't be being forgiven of your sins.

No, I probably wouldn't.

Katie: Why wouldn't you be forgiven of your sins without the sacrament? I thought that when we repent we are forgiven.

When we repent, we are forgiven, Katie. That is absolutely correct. But what is it that cleanses us from our sins? What is it that brings the Atonement into our lives, purifies our hearts, and sanctifies our souls?

Katie: I don't know. I always thought it was just the Atonement that did that.

Let's take a look at a few verses, shall we? Look at 2 Nephi 31:17.

Katie: I'll read that. It says, "Wherefore, do the things which I have told you I have seen that your Lord and your Redeemer should do; for, for this cause have they been shown unto me, that ye might know the gate by which ye should enter. For the gate by which ye should enter is repentance and baptism by water; and then cometh a remission of your sins by fire and by the Holy Ghost."

107

Notice in that verse the process: Faith, repentance, baptism, Holy Ghost. Which one of those remits or takes away our sins?

 Katie: It says, "then cometh a remission of your sins by fire and by the Holy Ghost." So it is receiving the Holy Ghost that cleanses us from sin?

Yes, it is. Elder Bruce R. McConkie taught that "the Holy Ghost is the Sanctifier."[5] It is through His power that men may be sanctified and washed clean from all sin. Elder D. Todd Christofferson taught that the Holy Ghost "is the messenger of grace by which the blood of Christ is applied to take away our sins and sanctify us."[6] Look what Jesus taught about this great truth in 3 Nephi 27:20.

 Lindsay: I've got that one: "Now this is the commandment: Repent, all ye ends of the earth, and come unto me and be baptized in my name, that ye may be sanctified by the reception of the Holy Ghost, that ye may stand spotless before me at the last day." So it says that same thing: Repent, get baptized, and receive the Holy Ghost, and the Holy Ghost will sanctify you.

That is right. The Holy Ghost is the purifier or the cleanser. That is what the word *sanctify* means. And when do we hear that word "sanctify" all the time?

 David: In the sacrament prayer. I have it memorized. The priests bless the bread and water to "sanctify [them] to the souls of all those who partake of it" (D&C 20:77).

Good, David. We hear that sacrament prayer each week, but let's see if we really know what it says. As we partake of the sacrament and renew our covenants, we make three specific promises, and God promises us something in return. What is it that we promise?

Katie: That we are willing to take upon us the name of Christ.

Good, that's one. What else?

 Trevor: That we are willing to keep Christ's commandments.

Excellent. One more:

 Justin: That we will always remember Him.

Great. And what is the promised blessing?

 Olivia: That we will always have His Spirit to be with us.

So, implied in that promise to always have the Spirit with us—if we keep our end of the covenant—is that the Spirit will cleanse us and sanctify our souls from sin as we receive him. You see how that works? It is almost like the sacrament is the final element in the repentance and cleansing process. Elder D. Todd Christofferson called baptism—and therefore the sacrament, which renews baptism—"the culminating step, the capstone of our repentance."[7]

 Mikayla: But don't you have to be worthy to take the sacrament? Not just anyone can take it and have their sins taken away. I've always had a hard time knowing if I am worthy enough to take the sacrament because we aren't supposed to take it if we aren't worthy. Is that right?

That is a great question, Mikayla, and a common one that many of us have. You're right—we aren't supposed to take the sacrament if we aren't worthy. Christ specifically forbade it when he said, "For whoso eateth and drinketh my flesh and blood unworthily eateth and drinketh damnation to his soul; therefore if ye know that a man is unworthy to eat and drink of my flesh and blood ye shall forbid him" (3 Nephi 18:29). Those are pretty pointed words from our Savior. He is serious about us not taking the sacrament unworthily. So how do we know if we are worthy to partake of it?

David: Well, we should think of the covenant we are making and ask ourselves these questions: Am I willing to keep the commandments? Am I willing to take the name of Christ upon me? Am I willing to always remember Him? I think if we can honestly answer yes to those questions, then we are ready to take it.

That is great insight, David, thanks. Let's turn to the book *True to the Faith* and see what it teaches.

Lindsay: I'll read it. It says: "In preparation for the sacrament each week, take time to examine your life and repent of your sins. You do not need to be perfect in order to partake of the sacrament, but you should have a spirit of humility and repentance in your heart. Every week you should prepare for that sacred ordinance with a broken heart and a contrite spirit (see 3 Nephi 9:20)."[8]

Katie: So it looks like as long as we are repenting of our sins, we are fine to take the sacrament, right?

Repentance is the key there, as Katie said.

Justin: So people can commit some serious sin on Friday night, confess on Saturday, and take the sacrament to be cleansed of it on Sunday?

Not really. That isn't the way it works. Remember, repentance isn't only confession. Repentance can be defined in one word: Change.

Specifically, change toward God.[9] So if I truly desire to repent, then I will desire to and begin to change my life through the Atonement of Jesus Christ. That kind of change doesn't happen overnight. Some sins, especially serious ones, usually take longer periods of time to overcome.

 Lindsay: Well, and if you are involved in big sins then you would talk to your bishop about them, right? And if he didn't feel like you were ready to take the sacrament, he would tell you not to.

 Katie: Why would your bishop not want you to take the sacrament if you had confessed to him and were trying to repent?

 David: Well, I think it is back to the covenant. Can someone who is involved in serious sins, like someone who broke the law of chastity over the weekend, really say that they are ready to make a covenant to be willing to keep the commandments and always remember Christ the next day? The bishop probably would want to see that you have begun to change and are willing to keep the covenant, and won't just go break it again the next day.

That's a good thought, David. Keep in mind, Katie, that if partaking of the sacrament is a critical element in the repentance process, the bishop will want to ensure that you have godly sorrow, have abandoned the sin, and have begun to live righteously. The Lord has said, "By this ye may know if a man repenteth of his sins—behold, he will confess them and forsake them" (D&C 58:43). As the authorized judge of the ward, when the bishop sees that someone is truly repentant, he will authorize them to take the sacrament, renew their covenants through the sacrament, and begin to receive the cleansing and purifying effect of the Holy Ghost.

 Mikayla: So, as long as I have faith, repent, and am ready to keep the covenants of the sacrament, I am worthy to take it?

That's right. Elder John H. Groberg summarized it well when he taught:

"What does it mean to partake of the sacrament worthily? Or how do we know if we are unworthy?

"If we desire to improve (which is to repent) and are not under priesthood restriction, then, in my opinion, we are worthy. If, however, we have no desire to improve, if we have no intention of following the guidance of the Spirit, we must ask: Are we worthy to partake, or are we making a mockery of the very purpose of the sacrament, which is to act as a catalyst for personal repentance and improvement? . . .

"The sacrament is an intensely personal experience, and we are the ones who knowingly are worthy or otherwise."[10]

 Mikayla: That is a great quote. It makes so much sense.

You see, this process we should go through each week in preparation for the sacrament is the "righteous cycle" I mentioned earlier: Have faith, repent, reconnect myself to Christ through covenant, get rebaptized through the sacrament, and receive the Holy Ghost. It looks like this:

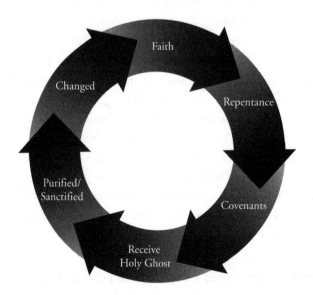

As we go through this righteous cycle we not only are purified and sanctified by the Holy Ghost, but we are eventually *changed* to become like Christ. The ultimate purpose of the righteous cycle is to connect us to Christ through covenant, and to help us *become* like Christ through the infinite Atonement and cleansing power of the Holy Ghost. Elder Dallin H. Oaks said: "The gospel of Jesus Christ is the plan by which we can become what children of God are supposed to become. This spotless and perfected state will result from a *steady succession* of covenants, ordinances, and actions."[11] The scriptures say we have to be changed if we want to be with Christ in heaven. The scriptures call this being "born again" (John 3:3).

Justin: Born again? I thought that was just the name of an evangelical group or something.

Well, we thought that grace was just "a Christian thing" as well, didn't we? No, we all need to be born again. Why don't you go ahead and read John 3:3 for us?

Justin: "Jesus answered and said unto him, Verily, verily, I say unto thee, Except a man be born again, he cannot see the kingdom of God." So what does that mean, to "be born again"?

The book *True to the Faith* has a good summary. Let's read from there under "conversion," which is another word the scriptures use to describe the process of being born again. What does it mean to *convert* something?

Trevor: It means to change it. Like changing a transformer from a car into a robot. Or, like converting a fraction into a decimal—that was for Mikayla.

Mikayla: Impressive—for a football player.

Trevor, will you read that section under "Conversion" in *True to the Faith* from the beginning all the way down through the verse in Mosiah?

Trevor: "To be able to receive the blessing of eternal life . . . we need to change. More accurately, we need to *be changed,* or converted, through the power of the Savior's Atonement and through the power of the Holy Ghost. This process is called conversion.

"Conversion includes a change in behavior, but it goes beyond behavior; it is a change in our very nature. It is such a significant change that the Lord and His prophets refer to it as a rebirth, a change of heart, and a baptism of fire. The Lord said:

"'Marvel not that all mankind, yea, men and women, all nations, kindreds, tongues and people, must be born again; yea, born of God, changed from their carnal and fallen state, to a state of righteousness, being redeemed of God, becoming his sons and daughters;

"'And thus they become new creatures; and unless they do this, they can in nowise inherit the kingdom of God' (Mosiah 27:25–26)."[12]

So it says that Christ wants us to become "new creatures," or changed. What does Christ want us to change?

Trevor: He wants us to change the things that aren't like Him. He wants us to become like He is.

David: He wants us to change the "natural man." It is like that scripture mastery verse, Mosiah 3:19.

Quote it for us, my friend. What does it say?

David: "For the natural man is an enemy to God, and has

been from the fall of Adam, and will be, forever and ever, unless he yields to the enticings of the Holy Spirit, and putteth off the natural man and becometh a saint through the atonement of Christ the Lord, and becometh as a child, submissive, meek, humble, patient, full of love, willing to submit to all things which the Lord seeth fit to inflict upon him, even as a child doth submit to his father."

Notice that it is by the "enticings of the Holy Spirit . . . through the atonement" that our natural man is changed, or converted, and we are born again. The key is to let the Holy Ghost apply the Atonement to our lives, soften our hearts, and change our natural man into a spiritual man. The spiritual man is so opposite of the natural man that it takes a complete change—a complete turnabout toward God.

 Trevor: It is kind of like when I learned how to play basketball. As a kid, I shot two-handed so I could push the ball up to the ten-foot rim. I got pretty good shooting two-handed. Until one day, my dad came out and told me that it was time for me to start shooting the right way, with one hand balancing the ball on the side and the other hand primarily doing the shooting and follow-through, one-handed. Suddenly, I couldn't even get it up to the rim. It was horrible. I wanted to stay my old two-handed way, but my dad told me if I ever wanted to play in high school I had to learn it right, otherwise I wouldn't be good enough. Eventually, after a lot of work and practice, I figured it out and got good at it, and it made me into a much better shooter. Maybe changing from the natural man to the spiritual man is a lot like that.

That is a great analogy, Trevor. It is interesting that you said the word *eventually.* How long did it take you before you felt comfortable and were good at shooting one-handed?

Trevor: Like a year or two, at least.

Keep that in mind as we discuss how the righteous cycle changes us, converts us, and helps us become more Christlike. It doesn't happen overnight. Lindsay, you've changed from a little baby into a fairly tall girl. When did you become 5'9"? On what day?

 Lindsay: Well, it wasn't on a certain day. You know that.

Or, Dirk, when did you get your facial hair? What day?

 Dirk: January 27th, right when I turned sixteen. Just kidding. I still don't have enough facial hair to grow the kind of beard I want. Just a sweet little soul patch for now.

Maybe you'll keep changing, Dirk, slowly. You guys get the point. Change, especially changing our spiritual natures and becoming Christlike, is something that happens over time, not overnight. Elder D. Todd Christofferson taught: "You may ask, Why doesn't this mighty change happen more quickly with me? You should remember that the remarkable examples of King Benjamin's people, Alma, and some others in scripture are just that—remarkable and not typical. For most of us, the changes are more gradual and occur over time. Being born again, unlike our physical birth, is more a process than an event."[13]

Since it takes so much time is the reason why we need to be continually valiant in our testimony of Christ, and continually participating in the righteous cycle of faith, repentance, making covenants, receiving the Holy Ghost, being sanctified by its reception, and thus being changed—little by little. Each time we participate in this process, we become more and more like Christ, and our natural man is converted into a spiritual man—and we are "born again."

 Katie: So that is why we need to take the sacrament each week, so we do this righteous cycle on a consistent basis, and gradually, week by week, become like Christ?

That's right. The sacred sacrament is such a critical part of being born again because without it we cannot always have the Spirit to be with us to purify and change us. What the Lord wants to see is that, through enduring to the end in the righteous cycle, we have become like Him—that we have received His image in our countenances (see Alma 5:14). When we die and face the Lord at the Judgment, He will want to see what we have *become*. He wants to see if we are still a natural man, or a spiritual man, born once physically, and born again spiritually. If through baptism, the sacrament, and other ordinances we will have joined ourselves with Christ and become like Him, then He will claim us as His spiritual children, perfect us, and lead us right into heaven. If we have made continual covenants with Him in the righteous cycle and become more and more like Him, then we have great hope through Jesus at the final judgment.

CLASS #11

Hope through Jesus at Judgment

We began these classes by talking about what we think would happen if we died today and were brought before the final judgment to be placed in an eternal kingdom. I'm curious how you guys picture that moment of the final judgment.

 Katie: I've always pictured the final judgment like a movie, ya know? Where God will call my number—"Number 16,446,768,459" and I'm like, "Oh, that's me!"—and I'll sit down with Him and watch the movie of my life. It would start when I'm eight years old and go through every year since then.

 Justin: That's a long movie. Hope there is at least some celestial popcorn.

 Mikayla: Yeah, I've always thought the same thing, except when we watch the movie, that there are certain blank spots, or areas where the film of our life has been edited or cut out or something because we have repented, and the scriptures say that the Lord won't bring up the sins we've repented of.

Katie and Mikayla, thanks for your thoughts and insights. Mikayla, you are right, the Lord did say in D&C 58:42 that when we repent of our sins He will "remember them no more." But I have a question about why you think we would watch a film of our lives?

Katie: Well, I don't think it will be an actual film, but just that God will review our lives and see what good we have done and what evil we have done, or at least haven't repented of.

Now why would God do that? Why would He want to review all the good and evil we've done?

 Dirk: Can I step in? I've always thought of the final judgment like we are in a giant courtroom, only God is the judge and we are on trial. And, you know, in the courtroom is that gold blind lady holding the scales of justice.

 Katie: She's not blind, Dirk, she's blindfolded. It's to symbolize her fairness in not judging based on appearance.

 Dirk: Yeah, that blindfolded lady. Well, every time we do something good on earth, a little drop is made on the good side of the scales. And every time we do something naughty, a drop goes on the bad side. If we do big righteous things, then we get a big ol' drop onto the righteous scales. If we do big wicked monkey stuff, then a big drop goes onto the wicked side.

And if the righteous side outweighs the other . . .

 Dirk: Then God shouts out, "We've got a winner!" and lets us into heaven.

 Katie: I don't quite see it like that with the scales and all, but that is why I think God will review our life: He wants to see kind of a sum total of our good and bad acts.

I appreciate your comments, but I'm not sure that is how it will be. Here is why I say that: How does the situation you have just described mesh with what we have just learned about being "born again," and, especially, how does it mesh with what we have learned about *covenants?* For example, if using the blindfolded scales of justice were how we were really judged, what about those who live their whole life in sin, and then realize the error of their ways, come unto Christ, get baptized, make covenants, and then die? They might have one hundred thousand drops on the sin side of the scales, and only four big ones— faith, repentance, baptism, and the Holy Ghost—on the good side. So will they not go to the celestial kingdom? Or what about those who are righteous their whole lives, and rack up one hundred thousand righteous deeds because of all the good they have done, and then toward the end of their life they turn apostate, fall away from the Church, quit making and keeping covenants in the righteous cycle, rebel, and die in their sins? After a lifetime of righteousness they would have way more drops on the righteous side than their last few years on the wicked side. So should they go to the celestial kingdom?

 Trevor: Yeah, like Judas Iscariot, the member of the Twelve who betrayed Christ. He was righteous and then turned evil at the end.

Right. So if his righteous acts outweigh his evil acts, do we have a heavenly "winner"? That doesn't make sense, does it?

 Dirk: No, it doesn't. See, that is why you don't have blindfolded people doin' the judging . . .

It has nothing to do with blindfolds, my friend, although after what I'm about to say, you might wish that God really will be blindfolded at the Judgment. You see, I think the heart of the final judgment is a *clothing* question—a question of who will appear before God uncovered, and who will appear before Him clothed.

 Mikayla: Huh? The final judgment is a clothing question? I know modesty is important, but I didn't think that modesty will determine our eternal destiny.

Justin: Yeah, and what's up with what you're saying that we might not have clothes at the final judgment? That is like public humiliation number one.

Being naked in public could truly be the ultimate embarrassment. I mean, how many of us have had that horrible dream where for some reason we realize—in front of everyone—we are missing our clothes?

 Trevor: That isn't just a dream—that is a nightmare. I hope it never comes true and happens to me.

Well, it might happen to some. Metaphorically, some may find themselves naked at the final judgment. Let me show you what I mean by that: When Adam and Eve partook of the forbidden fruit and were in danger of being cast out of the Garden of Eden, the scriptures say that they went and hid themselves from God. Why do you think they did that?

 Justin: Because maybe they were ashamed of what they had done. You know, they felt bad about it and didn't want to get caught.

But they did get "caught," so to speak, because, come on, can you really hide from God? He knows and sees all! Look what Adam says to God when he finally comes out from the bushes in Genesis 3:9-10:

"And the Lord God called unto Adam, and said unto him, Where art thou?

"And he said, I heard thy voice in the garden, and I was afraid, because I was naked; and I hid myself."

So why did they hide?

 Lindsay: Because they were ashamed of what they had done and realized that they were naked.

You are right, Lindsay, they were ashamed. John the Revelator mentioned this same idea by connecting sin, nakedness, and shame in Revelation 16:15. Who wants to read it?

Olivia: I will. It says, "Behold, I come as a thief. Blessed is he that watcheth, and keepeth his garments, lest he walk naked, and they see his shame."

In the case of Adam and Eve, the word used is that they were *afraid* because they were naked. Other than the words *shame* or *afraid,* if you had to summarize into one word how it might feel to be unclothed in public, or worse, in front of God such as Adam or Eve, what words come to your mind?

Katie: Well, I think of the word *embarrassed.* You know, just the embarrassment that would come.

Trevor: I thought of the word *humiliation.* There is nothing worse than being caught doing something wrong . . . well . . . except being caught and missing your clothes.

David: I think of the word *exposed,* like there is nothing to hide behind.

Yes, *exposed* is a great word connected to nakedness. That is a good word to link the idea of nakedness to the final judgment. You see, just as with the example we read of Adam and Eve, there is a metaphorical relationship between nakedness and sin. Not that we will literally stand naked but in the sense that in front of God, or in His holy presence, our sins make us feel naked or exposed. Look how Alma uses the word *exposed* in Alma 34:16 when referring to the final judgment:

David: He says in that verse that those who do not exercise faith in Jesus Christ and repent of their sins will be "*exposed*

to the whole law of the demands of justice" (Alma 34:16; emphasis added) at the final judgment.

That is right. Our sins will make us feel exposed before God. "Naked" is even how the Book of Mormon prophet Jacob says it. Turn to 2 Nephi 9:14. Who will read just the first line of that scripture?

 Justin: I will. It says, "Wherefore, we shall have a perfect knowledge of all our guilt, and our uncleanness, and our nakedness."

Now I don't know if Jacob necessarily means that at the final judgment we will remember every little thing we ever did wrong, or if he is just saying that we will all have a perfect understanding of how unworthy and unclean we are to enter the kingdom of God. Either way, one thing is clear: in our sins, and with a perfect understanding of our guilt, we will feel figuratively naked, just like Adam and Eve physically did before God. And when we feel naked, what will we want more than anything?

 Katie: Um, to get out of there. To hide like Adam and Eve did.

Yes, I think we will want to hide. But, unfortunately, just as our first parents discovered, it is impossible to hide from God, and all of us will be required to stand before Him at the final judgment. Let's read what Alma the Younger said in Alma 12:14–15 about wanting to hide from God at the final judgment.

 Trevor: I'll read it.
"For our words will condemn us, yea, all our works will condemn us; we shall not be found spotless; and our thoughts will also condemn us; and in this awful state we shall not dare to look up to our God; and we would fain be glad if we

could command the rocks and the mountains to fall upon us to hide us from his presence.

"But this cannot be; we must come forth and stand before him in his glory, and in his power, and in his might, majesty, and dominion."

So back to the question: Since we can't hide from God, and we are metaphorically standing naked in front of Him in our sins at the final judgment, what will we want more than anything?

Olivia: To get something to cover us up.

Exactly. We will want to cover our nakedness and our shame and guilt with something more than a few fig leaves. We will want a coat! Now the good news is that, at the judgment bar, not all will be found naked; some will have been handed coats to cover themselves.

Dirk: Like from someone who works at a celestial Deseret Industries?

More like a celestial Salvation Army. Let's read the second half of that verse we left off back in 2 Nephi 9:14. Jacob teaches us who will have clothing to cover them. Dirk, will you do the honors?

Dirk: "And the righteous shall have a perfect knowledge of their enjoyment, and their righteousness, being clothed with purity, yea, even with the robe of righteousness." So it's the righteous who will be covered and not be naked? Man, I'd better step it up if I don't want to get humiliated!

Again, we're not talking about literal nakedness, but at the judgment bar, it is the righteous who will be "covered." So the question is, who covers them, and with what will they be covered?

David: Well, if we have learned anything from our discussions, I am positive it will be our Savior Jesus Christ who covers us. He is the one who saves us. He is the one who paid for our sins. He is the one who did the perfect Atonement. It makes sense that He will be the one to cover the righteous at the judgment bar.

Great comment, David. And, yes, you are right. It is Jesus who covers our nakedness, just as it was Jesus who covered Adam and Eve's nakedness and made "coats of skins, and clothed them" (Genesis 3:21). Elder Russell M. Nelson taught a really cool thing about what the word *atonement* means, and it is directly connected to this idea of being naked and being clothed. He said: "Rich meaning is found in study of the word *atonement* in the Semitic languages of Old Testament times. In Hebrew, the basic word for atonement is *kaphar,* a verb that means 'to cover' or 'to forgive.'"[1]

So another meaning of the word atonement is "to cover," or to cover up.

Mikayla: I think I get it. At the judgment bar, when we are all feeling naked and shameful because of the sins that we have all committed, Jesus' Atonement will "cover" up our sins. So it's like He is covering up our faults and wrapping us in a blanket of righteousness.

Yes! Isn't that a beautiful image to picture in your mind? Seeing Jesus come toward you in your shame to wrap you up, covering all your shortcomings and imperfections and sins, and clothing you in *His* righteousness? Oh, it is a beautiful and comforting thought to me! The scriptures testify that the righteous will "be clothed upon" by Jesus (D&C 29:13; 109:76). The Apostle Paul also comforted us by saying, "Being clothed [by Christ] we shall not be found naked" (2 Corinthians 5:3) at the judgment bar.

Katie: So can we assume that some people won't be covered by Christ? I mean, this whole time we have been studying about what it takes to get into the celestial kingdom and—

And what have you learned, Katie? Who do you think will get covered, and will there be some that aren't covered? Answer your own question, sister.

Katie: Well, from what we've learned I think that those who get covered will be those who took Christ's name on themselves here on earth. If we take His name on us through covenant, and we continue to put His name on us through covenant our whole lives, then I think Christ will put His name on us at the judgment and cover us with His Atonement.

Katie, what you just said is so interesting. What do you mean by "Christ will put His name on us at the judgment and cover us?" Do you mean He'll *claim* us because of our covenants with Him?

Katie: Yeah, I guess you could use the word *claim*.

Did you guys ever do that when you were younger—claim stuff? For instance, if you were getting up to leave the room, did you ever say, "I claim this spot . . . it's mine. Don't take it!" or when Mom would bake cookies, did you point to the biggest one and say, "This one's mine. I claim it"?

Lindsay: Man, with my brothers hoggin' everything, I still have to claim food all the time at my house. When we have dinner, if I don't claim a roll or something, they're gone and I go hungry. I gotta claim what is mine before someone else does.

Right on. We claim lots of stuff. Food, possessions, places, and even people. Now, keeping that in mind, let's read these verses from

Alma and see if Katie was right in saying that Christ will claim those who have exercised faith, repented, been baptized, received the Holy Ghost, and endured in the righteous cycle by continuing to make covenants and linking themselves with Christ. Go to Alma 42:22–24. Katie, let's see how right you were about this idea of Christ claiming His covenant people at the judgment.

Katie: "Which repentance, mercy claimeth; otherwise, justice claimeth the creature and executeth the law, and the law inflicteth the punishment; . . .

" . . . mercy claimeth the penitent, and mercy cometh because of the atonement. . . .

"For behold, justice exerciseth all his demands, and also mercy claimeth all which is her own; and thus, none but the truly penitent are saved."

So there are *two* sides claiming people at the judgment, not just one. Who, or *what*, are the two sides?

David: You would think it would be God and Satan, good and evil, or heaven and hell. But it isn't. Jesus has already saved everyone from death to be judged. It is only God who does the judging, and Satan has no power. The two sides claiming people at the judgment aren't God and Satan. Satan is out of the picture. The two sides claiming people are God and God. God's *mercy* and God's *justice.*

Well reasoned, David. So here is the question of all questions: As we stand there metaphorically naked in our sins and having a perfect knowledge of our shortcomings and imperfections, do we want mercy to claim us at the judgment bar, or do we want justice to claim us? Do we want God to be perfectly just and give us exactly what we deserve, or do we want Him to extend to us some mercy?

Mikayla: My vote is for mercy.

 Dirk: I'll speak for the whole world, bro. I think we all want some mercy.

I am sure we all will want mercy. Unfortunately, some will be claimed by justice. At the final judgment, some will stand there naked in their sins, fully exposed to the law of eternal justice, with a perfect knowledge of all their guilt and shame. They will see that they, on their own merits, are unworthy of the celestial kingdom and God's presence, that they have broken laws and violated commandments and are guilty of sin and therefore liable to pay the price of suffering for those sins. They will beg for mercy. But, sadly, they won't receive it.

 Mikayla: But that is sad! Why won't they receive mercy? Why won't Christ cover them?

It is sad, Mikayla. But what is sadder is that they rejected Christ and His Atonement when they could have accepted it. And because they rejected the Atonement, the Atonement cannot cover them. Christ's name isn't on them. They aren't on His team, so Christ can't claim them. They never came unto Christ when they had the chance, so Christ cannot come unto them with His mercy to save them from justice because they haven't qualified for it. Christ can't violate eternal laws and extend mercy to those who didn't follow what was required to qualify for His atoning mercy. Look how Alma said it in Alma 42:25. Mikayla, go ahead and read that for us.

 Mikayla: "What, do ye suppose that mercy can rob justice? I say unto you, Nay; not one whit. If so, God would cease to be God." So those people who don't qualify for the Atonement to cover them will be all on their own?

Yes, fully exposed and all on their own with nobody to save them because they have already rejected the One who is mighty to save. That is why in D&C 19 Jesus literally pleads with us to repent and come unto Him so He can cover us, so we don't have to be on our own. Read it with me. In verses 16-17 Jesus says, "I, God, have suffered these things for all, that they might not suffer *if they would repent; but if they would not repent they must suffer even as I*" (emphasis added). In many parts of the Book of Mormon it teaches that those who reject Jesus and don't make covenants with Him will be on their own at the judgment bar. The phrase the prophets used over and over again is that it's "as though there had been no redemption made" (Alma 12:18; see also Mosiah 16:5; Alma 11:41; Moroni 7:38). These poor people who rejected Jesus' Atonement, who refused to become part of His family through faith, repentance, and the new covenant, will longingly look to Jesus when they realize—too late—that they are on their own. Just as the foolish virgins, they will cry to Him at that awful moment of judgment and say, "Lord, Lord, open to us" (Matthew 25:11), or, using our analogy, "Lord, Lord, please cover me! Please wrap your Atonement around me and cover my shame!" And the Lord will sadly answer them, "Verily I say unto you, I know you not" (Matthew 25:12), or in other words, "You are not part of my family. I am sorry. You are not children of the covenant. Therefore, we are not linked. You didn't take my name on you, and so I cannot claim you as mine. Justice must claim you, and I cannot rob justice. Unfortunately, you are on your own." Then, as the scriptures say, there will be weeping and wailing and gnashing of teeth, as those who are filthy remain filthy still (see 2 Nephi 9:16; Mormon 9:14) and are sent to a lesser kingdom.

 Justin: And what about us? Since we aren't perfect and have sins, is that what will happen to us?

That is what this whole discussion has been about, Justin—what will happen to those of us who have made covenants before we get to the final judgment bar. Will we make it into the celestial kingdom, or will we be among the weepers and wailers and teeth-gnashers? My good brother, and all you good youth of Zion, this is my testimony about what will happen to us as people of the covenant:

Similar to those we have just spoken about, we also will stand before God at the judgment bar. Our sins will be fully exposed, our uncleanliness obvious to God and His holy angels, and especially to ourselves. We will have a perfect understanding that, on our own, we are unfit for the kingdom of God—that we are stained with sin and unqualified for God's holy presence and kingdom. Just as eternal justice is about to claim us and send us to a lesser kingdom, away from God's presence because of our unworthiness, someone will step in on our behalf. A mediator will step in. Or better yet, an advocate. Do you guys know what an advocate is?

 Katie: It is like a lawyer—someone who argues your case for you.

Yes, exactly. And who will our advocate be at the final judgment? Who will step in and plead our case before God?

 Justin: Jesus Christ will.

Yes, for the faithful children of the covenant, He will. We referred to this earlier, but with our added understanding, let's turn again to D&C 45:3–5 to read some of the most poetic, beautiful, and hopeful words in all of scripture. Who wants the privilege of reading these for us? Who wants to hear exactly what Christ will step in and say for those who are faithfully connected to Him by covenant?

 Olivia: Can I please?

Go ahead. Stand still, class, and listen to the salvation of God (see Exodus 14:13).

 Olivia: Christ says,
"Listen to him who is the advocate with the Father, who is pleading your cause before him—
"Saying: Father, behold the sufferings and death of him

who did no sin, in whom thou wast well pleased; behold the blood of thy Son which was shed, the blood of him whom thou gavest that thyself might be glorified;

"Wherefore, Father, spare these my brethren that believe on my name, that they may come unto me and have everlasting life."

There. Do you see what our Savior will do for His covenant children? As we stand there guilty in our sins—far from perfect—Jesus will step in for the children of the covenant. At that critical moment, Jesus will rescue and save those of us who have exercised faith in His name, repented, been baptized, received the Holy Ghost, and endured to the end through a continual cycle of making and striving to keep covenants. He will cover our shame and nakedness and guilt "with the robe of [His] righteousness" (2 Nephi 9:14).

He will put his hand out and stop justice from claiming and executing an eternal punishment on us, and instead He will kindly clothe us with the "garments of salvation" (Isaiah 61:10). Jesus will encircle us "in the arms of safety" (Alma 34:16) and extend mercy toward us. In essence, He will say, "Father, spare this one. This one is with me. I am covering her. This one has my name on him. He is my child. He is linked to me by covenant. Therefore, I claim them. I know they are not perfect and have shortcomings. But Father, I suffered for them and their imperfections. They are repentant. I paid the price to justice already for their weaknesses and sins. My infinite righteousness is now their infinite righteousness, my goodness their goodness, my holiness their holiness. Therefore, please let these who have believed on my name enter into Our presence and into Our rest in the celestial kingdom."

And because the Father loves the Son, and justice honors Christ's atoning payment of sin, He will let us enter. And how will we feel? What will we do at that moment when Jesus literally saves us?

 Mikayla: Words wouldn't be enough. But I would hug Him and tell Him how much I love Him and how thankful I am for Him saving me.

Lindsay: I would feel overwhelmed, like I had just been rescued or something.

 David: I know what I would do: I would fall down at His feet and worship Him.

I think all of us would. I think at that moment, out of sheer humbling gratitude and love, we will bathe His feet with tears of thankfulness and cry out to Him, "My Lord and my God" (John 20:28).

Because of the covenants I have made with Jesus, I look forward to that Day of Judgment with the hope and anticipation of feeling His redeeming love and atoning power, and so should you. We shouldn't fear not being able to inherit the celestial kingdom because of our imperfections. Because Jesus was perfect, we don't have to be. We simply need to be connected to Him by covenant.

Do you feel that hope that comes through the Atonement of Jesus Christ and our covenants with Him?

 Katie: I do now. To be honest, before these lessons, I didn't. I always hated talking about the final judgment and who will get into the celestial kingdom because it made me feel guilty and feel despair. But after understanding what is really required to inherit the celestial kingdom, and understanding Jesus' Atonement more . . . I don't know . . . I just . . . I just feel hope now. For the first time, I feel like I can make it—that even though I'm not perfect—with Jesus I can make it. That is such a great feeling.

Katie, thank you for that testimony. You hit it right on: This is a gospel of hope, not despair! What about the rest of you? Would you mind sharing your thoughts or testimony about Christ and His Atonement and what you have learned or felt from this study?

 David: I will. I've learned that even though I'm not perfect, I can still go to heaven. I've always known that Jesus was my

132

Savior and believed that, but I think I have come to realize through our study what that really means—to be saved by Jesus. Even though you guys tease me that I will be a future prophet, I was one of the students who marked at the beginning of class that I would go to the terrestrial kingdom, because I always thought that I had to do everything exactly right, which I don't. I kind of thought I had to save myself through my own good works. I'm just so thankful that not only will Jesus save me from death, but that He will also save me from my imperfections and sins. I love Him so much for doing that and hope I can thank Him through a lifetime of service in His Church. And I say these things in the name of Jesus Christ, amen.

 Mikayla: Can I say something I've really come to learn? I've learned that I shouldn't get down on myself because I make mistakes. Sometimes I've felt like giving up on the gospel because I feel like I don't measure up—that I can't make it to heaven, so why try? I've always been one who wished I could start over again and have a clean slate. I'm so thankful that we discussed the importance of the sacrament and what it really can do in cleansing us on a weekly basis. I never—ever— want to miss a week of church and taking the sacrament. As a matter of fact, I wish it were Sunday today so I could go reconnect myself to Christ through covenant and renew my baptism and start fresh. Knowing this truth has helped increase my desire to always stay active in the Church, and not fall into inactivity and fall outside of the "righteous cycle" that we talked about. I know that if I can just stay actively engaged and keep making and keeping sacred covenants, that I can be saved in the celestial kingdom. I just want to bear my testimony that I know that Jesus' Atonement is real and that through Him we can be cleansed of our sins and be made pure and holy and fit for God's kingdom. And I say this in the name of Jesus Christ, amen.

 Justin: I guess I'll say something. I don't usually do this. As a matter of fact, I never have. But, anyway. What I took from our classes was that I need to be linked with Christ. Like in our basketball analogy that I did, shooting the ball and having it rebounded—that really hit me—the need to be linked or connected to Jesus through covenants, because if I am, then I can't lose. It makes me want to go to the temple one day and make more covenants with Him, because I want to be on Christ's team. I want to be with Him and have Him claim me in the next life as one of His sons. I know I can't lose if I'm with Jesus. I've never really told anyone this, but deep down inside I really want to serve a mission. I want to go out and tell other people about Christ and help them to make covenants with Him so He can save them, too. I believe that this Church is true, and that it has the true gospel. In the name of Jesus Christ, amen.

Thank you so much for those testimonies. God bless you good youth of Zion. The Lord loves you! Don't give up on yourselves, and don't give up on Jesus or lose hope in His ability to save. I want to close with my testimony to you: I love my Savior Jesus Christ. I love Him with all my heart. I love Him because of His perfect life, which made Him worthy to perform His perfect Atonement. I am thankful beyond any words I can express that Jesus overcame the fall of Adam and Eve, and conquered sin and death. I testify to you that Jesus did, in reality, pay the price of all our sins and in doing so satisfied the demands of justice for those who truly repent in His name. I testify that because of Him and His infinite Atonement, we can be forgiven of our sins, cleansed, purified, and sanctified. I have faith in Jesus' atoning grace. I know that even though I am far from perfect, and always will be during my mortal life, that Jesus' grace can cover my imperfections—that He can and will clothe me with His righteousness and cover my shame. I know that because of eternal covenants, I am linked with Jesus Christ. I know that if I am faithful to my covenants that Jesus will extend His perfection to cover my imperfection. I testify that we can all "come unto Christ, and be perfected in him" (Moroni 10:32)—that the celestial kingdom will be full of normal men and women "made perfect [by] Jesus the mediator of the new covenant" (D&C 76:69). I testify that because He was perfect, we don't have to be—that we don't have to qualify ourselves for the celestial kingdom, but instead qualify ourselves for Christ, and He will bring us into the celestial kingdom. We simply have to come unto the perfect Son of God, the Holy One of Israel. This is the testimony that is in me, and I leave it in the name of Him who is mighty to save, even Jesus Christ, amen.

ACKNOWLEDGMENTS

I am grateful to many for helping this book become a reality:

To my wife, Cindy, for her love of this topic, her faithful support and encouragement while I was writing, and her suggestions to make the manuscript better.

To my children, Lauren, Reagan, Jane, Eli, and Vivian, for sharing their dad's time so he could write another "Jesus" book.

To my sister and the real writer in the family, Angela Hallstrom, for her creative help regarding the book's characters, dialogue, and format.

To my good friends and colleagues John Hilton III and Brandon Gunnell for their insightful manuscript feedback and help in gathering survey responses.

To all those who read draft versions of this book, for their time and perspectives.

To Dr. Brent L. Top for his helpful doctrinal clarifications and suggestions.

To Richard Peterson and Lisa Mangum for their professional editing.

To Rachael Ward for her diligent work in typesetting the book, and to Richard Erickson and his design team for the cover, character avatars, and layout.

Finally, to Chris Schoebinger for his belief in me and his support for this project.

Thank you.

ENDNOTES

CLASS #1: THE QUESTION AND THE QUANDARY

1. Joseph Smith, *Teachings of the Prophet Joseph Smith,* sel. Joseph Fielding Smith (Salt Lake City: Deseret Book, 1976), 358.
2. Spencer W. Kimball, *The Teachings of Spencer W. Kimball,* ed. Edward L. Kimball (Salt Lake City: Bookcraft, 1982), 23.

CLASS #2: UNDERSTANDING "PERFECTION"

1. Russell M. Nelson, "Perfection Pending," *Ensign,* November 1995, 86.
2. Nelson, "Perfection Pending," 86; emphasis added.
3. Nelson, "Perfection Pending," 86.
4. See Joseph Smith, *History of The Church of Jesus Christ of Latter-day Saints,* ed., B. H. Roberts, 2d ed., 7 vols. (Salt Lake City: The Church of Jesus Christ of Latter-day Saints, 1932–51), 6:306–7; William H. Bennett, "Our Goal Is Perfection," *Ensign,* November 1976, 29.
5. Nelson, "Perfection Pending," 87.
6. Bruce R. McConkie, "The Probationary Test of Mortality," address given at the University of Utah Institute of Religion, 10 January 1982, 11; emphasis added.
7. Nelson, "Perfection Pending," 88.

CLASS #3: HEAVEN, HELL, AND DEGREES OF GLORY

1. Wilford Woodruff, in *Journal of Discourses,* 26 vols. (Liverpool: Latter-day Saints' Book Depot, 1854–86), 22:147.
2. Quentin L. Cook, "Our Father's Plan—Big Enough for All His Children," *Ensign,* May 2009, 37.

CLASS #4: THE TELESTIAL KINGDOM

1. See *For the Strength of Youth* (Salt Lake City: The Church of Jesus Christ of Latter-day Saints, 2001), 26.
2. See *For the Strength of Youth,* 28.
3. See Bruce R. McConkie, *Mormon Doctrine,* 2d ed. (Salt Lake City: Bookcraft, 1966), 520.
4. "The Family: A Proclamation to the World," *Ensign,* November 1995, 102.
5. LDS Bible Dictionary, s.v. "Hell," 700.

6. John A. Widtsoe, *Message of the Doctrine and Covenants* (Salt Lake City: Bookcraft, 1969), 167.

CLASS #5: THE TERRESTRIAL KINGDOM

1. Bruce R. McConkie, "The Seven Deadly Heresies," in *Speeches of the Year, 1980* (Provo: Brigham Young University Press, 1981), 77–78.
2. Joseph Fielding Smith, in Conference Report, April 1969, 122; emphasis added.
3. See Theodore M. Burton, in Conference Report, April 1964, 72.
4. Spencer W. Kimball, *The Teachings of Spencer W. Kimball,* ed. Edward L. Kimball (Salt Lake City: Bookcraft, 1982), 50.
5. *Gospel Principles Lesson Handbook* (Salt Lake City: The Church of Jesus Christ of Latter-day Saints, 1992), 297–98.

CLASS #6: THE CELESTIAL KINGDOM

1. See also Bruce R. McConkie, *The Millennial Messiah* (Salt Lake City: Deseret Book, 1982), 661.
2. Quentin L. Cook, "Our Father's Plan—Big Enough for All His Children," *Ensign,* May 2009, 36.
3. Bruce R. McConkie, quoted in Robert L. Millet, *Within Reach* (Salt Lake City: Deseret Book, 1995), 10.
4. David A. Bednar, "Ye Must Be Born Again," *Ensign,* May 2007, 22.
5. See James E. Faust, "The Gift of the Holy Ghost—A Sure Compass," *Ensign,* May 1989, 31–33.
6. See Bruce R. McConkie, "Agency or Inspiration?" *New Era,* January 1975, 38.
7. See Russell M. Nelson, "Celestial Marriage," *Ensign,* November 2008, 92–95.
8. Spencer W. Kimball, *The Teachings of Spencer W. Kimball,* ed. Edward L. Kimball (Salt Lake City: Bookcraft, 1982), 297.
9. See *True to the Faith: A Gospel Reference* (Salt Lake City: The Church of Jesus Christ of Latter-day Saints, 2004), 115.
10. See Harold B. Lee, *The Teachings of Harold B. Lee,* ed. Clyde J. Williams (Salt Lake City: Bookcraft, 1996), 22.
11. "The Family: A Proclamation to the World," *Ensign,* November 1995, 102.
12. Russell M. Nelson, "Salvation and Exaltation," *Ensign,* May 2008, 8, 9.
13. Dallin H. Oaks, "'The Great Plan of Happiness,'" *Ensign,* November 1993, 75.

CLASS #7: THE PERFECT ATONEMENT

1. Ezra Taft Benson, "The Book of Mormon and the Doctrine and Covenants," *Ensign,* May 1987, 85.
2. See *True to the Faith: A Gospel Reference* (Salt Lake City: The Church of Jesus Christ of Latter-day Saints, 2004), 14–21.
3. See *True to the Faith,* 16.
4. Merrill J. Bateman, in Conference Report, April 1995, 16–17; emphasis added.
5. Jeffrey R. Holland, "None Were with Him," *Ensign,* May 2009, 88.
6. As quoted by James E. Faust, "The Atonement: Our Greatest Hope," *Ensign,* November 2001, 18. See also "Pres. Hinckley: Christmas a Result of Redeeming Christ," *Church News,* 10 December 1994, 4.

7. James E. Faust, "A Personal Relationship with the Savior," *Ensign,* November 1976, 58.

CLASS #8: AMAZING GRACE

1. http://www.nba.com/history/players/jordan_stats.html
2. LDS Bible Dictionary, s.v. "Grace," 697.
3. *For the Strength of Youth* (Salt Lake City: The Church of Jesus Christ of Latter-day Saints, 2001), 42.
4. In *Hymns of The Church of Jesus Christ of Latter-day Saints* (Salt Lake City: The Church of Jesus Christ of Latter-day Saints, 1985), no. 98.
5. LDS Bible Dictionary, s.v. "Grace," 697.

CLASS #9: JOINED WITH JESUS

1. D. Todd Christofferson, "The Power of Covenants," *Ensign,* May 2009, 20.
2. Christofferson, "The Power of Covenants," 20.
3. See David A. Bednar, "Honorably Hold a Name and Standing," *Ensign,* May 2009, 97–100.

CLASS #10: THE RIGHTEOUS CYCLE

1. Dallin H. Oaks, "The Aaronic Priesthood and the Sacrament," *Ensign,* November 1998, 38; emphasis added.
2. Boyd K. Packer, "Washed Clean," *Ensign,* May 1997, 9.
3. Jeffrey R. Holland, *Upon My Holy Day,* Doctrine and Covenants CES Video (Salt Lake City: The Church of Jesus Christ of Latter-day Saints, 2002).
4. Joseph Fielding Smith, *Church History and Modern Revelation,* 4 vols. (Salt Lake City: The Church of Jesus Christ of Latter-day Saints, 1946–1949), 1:123.
5. Bruce R. McConkie, "The Ten Blessings of the Priesthood," *Ensign,* November 1977, 33.
6. D. Todd Christofferson, "The Power of Covenants," *Ensign,* May 2009, 22.
7. D. Todd Christofferson, "Born Again," *Ensign,* May 2008, 78.
8. *True to the Faith: A Gospel Reference* (Salt Lake City: The Church of Jesus Christ of Latter-day Saints, 2004), 148.
9. See LDS Bible Dictionary, s.v. "Repentance," 760–61.
10. John H. Groberg, "The Beauty and Importance of the Sacrament," *Ensign,* May 1989, 38; emphasis added.
11. Dallin H. Oaks, "The Challenge to Become," *Ensign,* November 2000, 33; emphasis added.
12. *True to the Faith,* 40–41; emphasis in original.
13. Christofferson, "Born Again," 78.

CLASS #11: HOPE THROUGH JESUS AT JUDGMENT

1. Russell M. Nelson, "The Atonement," *Ensign,* November 1996, 34.

INDEX

Adam and Eve, 60–63, 121–22
Adultery, 27–29
Atonement: perfection and, 59–60;
   Fall and, 60–63; for sin, 63–67; for
   afflictions and temptations, 67–71;
   grace and, 73–87; infinite, 99–102;
   judgment and, 124–32

Baptism, 50–51, 91–96, 104–9
Bateman, Merrill J., 68
Bednar, David A., 103
Benson, Ezra Taft, 61

Celestial kingdom: worthiness for, 3–7;
   requirements for, 19–20, 49–58;
   description of, 34; number of people
   in, 46–49; perfection and, 59–60
Change, 113–16
Children, salvation of, 3
Christofferson, D. Todd: on baptism,
   96, 109; on covenants, 99; on Holy
   Ghost, 108; on change, 116
Commandments, 8–10, 51
Conversion, 113–16
Cook, Quentin L., 25, 48
Covenants, 91–99, 101–3, 126–32

Damnation, 42
Death, 62–63
Degrees of glory: compared to colleges,
   17–19; requirements for, 19–20; in
   New Testament, 23–24; salvation
   and, 24–25. *See also* Celestial

kingdom, Telestial kingdom, and
   Terrestrial kingdom
Dishonesty, 30–31

Effort, 85–87
Enduring to the end, 51–52, 103
Eternal progression, 44
Exaltation, 55–58

Faith, overcoming by, 51–52
Fall, 60–63
Faust, James E., 72
Fornication, 27–29

Gospel, principles and ordinances of,
   51–54
Grace: atonement and, 72–87;
   qualifying for, 88–103
Groberg, John H., 112

Heavenly Father, 12–13, 55–56, 127
Hell, 20–21, 33
Hinckley, Gordon B., 71
Holland, Jeffrey R., 69, 106
Holy Ghost, 2, 51, 108–9
Holy Spirit of promise, 53

Immorality, 27–29
Infinite atonement, 99–102
Israelites, 94–97

Jesus Christ: perfection and, 12–15;
   resurrection of mankind and, 22–23;
   testimony of, 49–50; love of, 71;
   becoming like, 116–17; judgment

and, 124–32. *See also* Atonement;
  Grace
Joshua, 97–98
Judgment: grace and, 85–87;
  perceptions of final, 118–20; hiding
  from, 120–25; being claimed at,
  126–32
Justice, 127–32

Kimball, Spencer W.: on unpardonable
  sin, 2; on eternal progression, 44;
  on temple marriage, 55

Laborers, parable of, 83
Life, 43–44
Love, of Jesus Christ, 71

Marriage, 44, 54–58
McConkie, Bruce R.: on salvation, 16,
  48; on terrestrial kingdom, 39; on
  Holy Ghost, 108
Mercy, 127–32
Moroni, 98–99
Mortality, 43–44
Murder, 29

Nakedness, 120–25
Nelson, Russell M.: on perfection, 9–10,
  11, 16; on Jesus Christ, 14; on
  exaltation, 56; on atonement, 125
Nephites, 13–14
New Testament, 23–24

Oaks, Dallin H.: on blessings in
  eternities, 57; on sacrament, 105;
  on salvation, 113
Outer darkness, 2

Packer, Boyd K., 105
Passover, 94–95
Perfection: commandment on, 6–7;
  understanding, 9–16; atonement
  and, 59–60, 72; through grace, 72,
  73–87; covenants and, 101–2

Plan of salvation, 32–33
Premortal existence, 32–33
Pride, 40

Rahab, 96–97
Repentance: for immorality, 28–29;
  atonement and, 65; sacrament and,
  104–11
Resurrection: perfection and, 13–15;
  of mankind, 22–25; last, 31;
  atonement and, 66
Righteous cycle, 112–17

Sacrament: renewing covenants
  through, 104–9; worthiness for,
  109–12; righteous cycle and,
  112–17
Salvation: degrees of glory and, 24–25;
  exaltation and, 55–58; through
  grace, 81–83, 89–90
Shame, 120–25
Sin: against Holy Ghost, 2; worthiness
  and, 4–7; atonement for, 63–67,
  71–72; sacrament and, 104–9;
  shame over, 121–26
Smith, Joseph, 2, 31–32
Smith, Joseph Fielding, 40, 106
Sower, parable of, 85
Spirit paradise, 21–22
Spirit prison, 21–22
Spirit world, 21–22
Suffering, 64–71

Talents, parable of, 84–85
Telestial kingdom, 25, 26–35
Temple ordinances, 103
Terrestrial kingdom, 3–4, 33–34, 36–45
Token, 95

Whoremonger, 27
Widtsoe, John A., 33
Woodruff, Wilford, 20
Works, 89–91

ANTHONY SWEAT is a full-time religious educator. He is the co-author of the bestselling book, *Why? Powerful Answers and Practical Reasons for Living LDS Standards,* published by Deseret Book. He and his wife, Cindy, are the parents of five children.

Why?
Powerful Answers and
Practical Reasons for
Living LDS Standards

By John Hilton III and
Anthony Sweat

Visit ldswhy.com

A web site community for LDS youth to share experiences, ask questions, and find answers!